RICHARD

RALPH ADAMS CRAM

RALPH ADAMS CRAM

American Medievalist

BY DOUGLASS SHAND TUCCI

BOSTON PUBLIC LIBRARY

MCMLXXV

© Copyright 1975 by Douglass Shand Tucci

COVER: In a poster of 1917 advertising Ralph Adams Cram's *The Substance of Gothic*, the title of the present essay on Cram and his work has been substituted for the original titling.

ILLUSTRATIONS: Please turn first to the pictorial survey following page 16.

... Those who have never fallen under the spell of Gothic, or have enjoyed it only romantically, may think that [Cram] talks romantic nonsense. But he does not enjoy Gothic romantically or talk romantic nonsense about it. He hears its living music, and it is to him not past but eternal.

> from a review of Ralph Adams Cram's
> *The Heart of Europe* in *The Times*
> (of London) *Literary Supplement*,
> 30 March 1916

It is doubtful if any product in the history of American architecture makes more compelling claim to this solicitude than that which lies to the account of Ralph Adams Cram and Bertram Grosvenor Goodhue. ... Cram has always been more than the architect. He has been a vital and developing force in the intellectual life of the nation. ... In the austere quality of his mind and the logical enterprise of his pencil one detects a resemblance to McKim as certainly as one perceives the analogy between Goodhue and Stanford White. ... As one reviews the long record of commissions from All Saints', Ashmont, to St. John The Divine, it seems a most fortuitous circumstance that Cram's philosophic leadership in the Gothic movement in America should have been paralleled by a professional accomplishment of such outstanding technical excellence. The artistic philosopher is not usually endowed with articulation in this order.

> Charles Donagh Maginnis,
> from the Introduction to
> *The Works of Cram and Ferguson*
> (New York), 1929

Among the scholars and interpreters of the Middle Ages, [Cram] was the artist and the creator. His was a rare and beautiful spirit.

> Professor George R. Coffman
> to Mr. John Nicholas Brown,
> 6 October 1942

Your nave is glorious—in its half built state I can see that it will realize much more than all the beauty I at once felt in the drawings. Your design surpasses what the Gothic builders achieved in their to me superlative effect—the vista through openings at openings beyond. If you can get the same inspired execution for the nave that you did for the baptistry, you will have written a tenth symphony.

> Professor A. Kingsley Porter
> to Ralph Adams Cram,
> 22 June 1926

FOREWORD

THIS first retrospective exhibition of the work of Ralph Adams Cram could scarcely have been attempted were it not for the generosity of Hoyle, Doran and Berry, the successor architects to Cram and Ferguson, and of Mrs. Mary Carrington Cram Nicholas and Mr. Ralph Adams Cram II. The architects have in the first place presented to the Library the considerable number of sketches, drawings, perspectives and correspondence of the Cram office that have survived in their archives in some cases for more than eighty-five years. Mr. Cram's daughter, Mrs. Nicholas, has subsequently greatly enriched this collection by giving to the Library through the cooperation of the successor architects an enormous amount of Ralph Adams Cram's manuscripts, letters and memorabilia. A smaller but hardly less significant collection has been given by Mr. Cram's grandson, Mr. Ralph Adams Cram II. A few sketches and cartoons of sculpture and glass in Cram churches have been used in this exhibition from the Connick, Evans and Burham collections.

The exhibition is co-sponsored not only by Hoyle, Doran and Berry, but by the Dean and Chapter of the Cathedral Church of St. John The Divine in New York, whose association with the Cram office is now nearly three-quarters of a century old. It will be mounted at the Cathedral Church following the Library showing.

The exhibition has been arranged and the catalogue prepared by Douglass Shand Tucci. We are indebted to him and to Mr. John T. Doran and to the Very Reverend James Parks Morton for their support.

PHILIP J. MCNIFF
Director, Boston Public Library

RALPH ADAMS CRAM
1863–1942

IF it is dangerous to take the measure of a man from his obituaries, their number and diversity as well as their content do usually yield the measure a man's *contemporaries* took of him—a significant fact his posterity is too seldom disinterested enough to inquire into very closely. This is unfortunate. Nothing is more ruinous to historical scholarship than to take the eulogists at their word— unless it is to automatically discount them—which our (alas) widespread habit of appraising one generation by the standards of another constantly encourages us to do. Yet one can no more despise a man's hagiographers than his detractors. One must take evidence from both, and from the obituary writer and (if the man is important enough, as Ralph Adams Cram was) the editorial editor who are caught between them. Nor is this only because the tale is so often found to be in the contrasts. Surely we are coming to see that too many art historians have cared more for art than for history, and that art historical scholarship no less than biography and history generally (where the idea is perhaps more traditional) must insist upon considering a man and his work on his own terms as well as by reference to those of his posterity. Ideally, this must involve re-creating the historical figure against the background of his own time before trying to assess his place in the longer perspective. Thus one notes carefully what was said of a man not because it seems now right, wrong, wise or foolish, but because it was said at all, and by whom: Franklin Roosevelt's public statement on the day of Cram's death that "a towering figure has been lost to our cultural life" is, for instance, chiefly significant for the fact that the then President of the United States felt it necessary to issue such a statement. Cram's obituaries (he died in 1942) may accordingly serve here as a more than merely convenient point of departure for this essay.[1]

There is, to be sure, nothing very surprising in the reports of his death in the religious press, unless one does not know that Cram was the man who of all men did "most to revive Catholic art in America" and that he and his principal artist-collaborator, Charles Connick, "revolutionized the appearance of ecclesiastical America." To some extent, the reports in the popular press are also less than startling. To read in the *Philadelphia Inquirer* that Cram was "world famous"; or that he was "known throughout the world" in the *Baltimore Sun*; or—to cite another variant of the same theme from the *New York World Telegram*—that he was "one of the world's foremost architects," only explains why thirty years later his name will usually still ring a bell, though which bell is another matter. More interesting, perhaps, is the remark in *Newsweek* that Cram was "one of our chief artistic crusaders": one wonders which crusade that was. What is perhaps most striking, however, is the frankness of editorial writers who it is clear by no means in every instance admired Cram. More surprising still, the most critical editorials nonetheless yield the most astonishing encomiums. The *Boston Globe*, for instance, noticed pointedly that Cram's first partner, Bertram Goodhue, may have been the better architect, but nevertheless admitted that Cram was so astounding a figure that "a writer of fiction would hesitate quite a while before venturing to invent such a career or such a person." "After every truthful, qualifying clause has been entered," allowed Uncle Dudley, "the fact remains that no architect in America has ever so succeeded in reaching the ear and the mind of the public. . . ." Yet the *Boston Herald* went further, and wondered what qualities enabled Cram "to maintain for decades an almost unique eminence among Americans of distinction." After this remarkable enough assertion, the editors volunteered the rather lame explanation that he was "a man of genius." The *Baltimore Sun* agreed. But here again, though, like the *Globe*, this journal felt bound to frankness, and reported that whether or not Cram was a great architect remained "a matter for debate," Baltimore (where by the way Cram built virtually nothing) no more than Boston could avoid in this case a still more remarkable encomium, remarkable too for its humility. "It is not easy to discuss Ralph Adams Cram . . . ," admitted the editors of the *Baltimore Sun*: "His genius was beyond the reach of ordinary processes of analysis"! Scarcely a comforting thought with which to undertake this essay, it is perhaps as well to have it before us here from the beginning.

One could go on—and, indeed, one can hardly not notice the *New York Times* editorial, where the editors conceded that "out of the richness of his mind, Mr. Cram has left an invaluable legacy of beauty that begins in New Hampshire and ends in San Francisco." Nor can one very well overlook the *Times* of London, where "the famous architect and authority on Gothic architecture" was significantly more interesting as "artist, philosopher and writer"—and in the last case as one who "wrote with knowledge and not merely with vague enthusiasm" on Gothic architecture, and who also "brought new light to bear on Japanese art and architecture." But though one might fill this essay with more of the same from both American and from foreign newspapers one could scarcely fill even a page (and here is what is startling) with the not only very brief but in one case even very curt notices accorded Cram in the architectural press! Alexander Hoyle, Cram's partner of many years, noticed this: "the popular press throughout the country," he wrote to a friend just after Cram's funeral, "gave a good deal of space to marking the end of this great career, but it is significant that very little attention has been paid to it by the architectural magazines."[2] But though Hoyle might have guessed the reason, both the question and whatever answer any might have made was quickly irrelevant, so swift was the decline of Cram's reputation after his death. Perhaps the nadir was marked by the comment of one writer only a few years ago that "Today [Cram] is only a bore."[3] Interestingly, however, the same writer warned in the same place that "Cram is so far out of date that there is a serious danger he may be revived before the century is over." That danger having now been realized somewhat beforehand—the phrase quoted here discloses, surely, how controversial Cram remains—the question Hoyle might have put in 1942 becomes now insistent. If Ralph Adams Cram, despite doubts as to his ability as an architect so widespread that they were reflected in his obituaries, really did maintain for decades "an almost unique eminence among Americans of distinction"; if his genius was actually so astonishing as to be "beyond the reach of ordinary processes of analysis"; why have we forgotten him so completely? Why are we only now rediscovering him? Why, moreover, did a distinguished scholar, in a generous review of a recent book of mine on Cram, conclude as well that our re-discovery was "inevitable"? Notwithstanding each generation's habit of perennially overthrowing the values and overlooking the accomplishments of their fathers, while at the same time discovering all over again those of their grandparents, I suspect the answer in every case is the answer Hoyle might have made thirty years ago to why an architect whose death was important enough to major American and foreign newspapers was apparently not very interesting to any of the architectural journals. And a discussion of this question is perhaps the best way in this early stage of our recovery of Cram to discover some at least of the significance of his life and work.

I. SCOPE

FUNDAMENTALLY, I think that his posterity—laymen and scholars alike—more or less instinctively concluded that Cram did too much. Indeed, it is perhaps the case that he wrote so much, built so much and influenced his time so variously and so improbably, that his posterity having inherited what amounted to a legend not unnaturally mistook it for a myth and promptly discounted it. The *Globe* after all was right: no novelist would dare to invent such a man as Cram. So also was the *Baltimore Sun*: Cram's life and work really are not susceptible to easy analysis. Scholars have therefore tended to choose less suspect and more obviously fruitful chores, and their avoidance of Cram has only in turn seemed to sanction the decline of his reputation.

Moreover, the *New York Times* encomium—New Hampshire to San Francisco—could as well be put "from Texas to Nova Scotia to Hawaii to Japan," and in any case points up the considerable difficulties of dealing at all intelligently with a man whose work will be found in almost every state in the union and abroad as well; whose church work alone (and many of the great churches of America are Cram's) amounts to over seventy cathedrals and churches in thirty-five states and two Canadian provinces; built by him not as is often thought just for Episcopalians (only forty of these seventy are Anglican) but also for Swedenborgians, Presbyterians, Unitarians, Baptists, Roman Catholics, Methodists, Orthodox, Lutherans and Congregationalists; and not just in gothic, but in every variety of it from Norman to Spanish, and in Byzantine, Lombard and Georgian as well. Nor can one overlook his houses or his office buildings or his libraries. And one certainly can't ignore his collegiate work, which includes important buildings at Wheaton, Richmond, Sweet Briar, University of Southern California, University of the South, Rollins, Notre Dame, Bryn Mawr, Williams, Rice Institute, Princeton and West Point—the last four of which he dominated—and in another dimension, a long tenure as Professor of the Philosophy of Architecture and head of the School of Architecture at the Massachusetts Institute of Technology. Furthermore, through his designs and through his writings, he led and virtually created the last phase of the American Gothic Revival. He was unarguably the foremost 20th century American Gothic polemicist. He inspired a wide-ranging new school of design and of decorative arts, and in the end he revolutionized the visual image of American Christianity in his time.

Not surprisingly, therefore, his correspondence abounds with letters of the sort written to Cram in 1938 by Joseph Hudnut, then Dean of the Graduate School of Design at Harvard, in which Hudnut allowed that "like all architects of my generation, I have been deeply influenced by your designs and writings."[4] But Cram's architecture, and his influence on the national architecture, can only be the beginning of any discussion of his work. For his two dozen books[5] and hundreds of scholarly and polemical articles and as many lectures, ranging in topic from British abbeys to Japanese temples, as often as not went far beyond the arts: one of his last and most widely read books, published in 1937, was entitled *The End of Democracy*, and Cram was by then so much a "household word" that neither in the book nor on the dust jacket did his publishers find it necessary to include any "about the author." Architect, theologian, liturgist, philosopher, medievalist, historian, social theorist, Cram founded or edited (often both) five journals, wrote for all the leading journals, including *The American Mercury* and the *Atlantic Monthly*, was a founder of the Medieval Academy of America, and though not Roman Catholic, was the foremost Catholic polemicist in this country. In sum, he exercised a wider influence on diverse and important aspects of the national culture than any other architect in our history. It is thus scarcely surprising that most scholars, amazed enough by the extent and diversity of his architecture, back away at once from the larger Cram, who is an astonishingly interdisciplinary figure. Even if the "causes" appeal, the enormousness of Cram's achievement is scarcely credible and suggests at once that he cannot have done many or even any of these things well enough to warrant serious inquiry. But if this was the case he successfully deluded quite a large number of people.

Many Anglicans, predictably, thought Cram not only the great religious architect of the world but the foremost ecclesiologist of the Anglican Communion.[6] But what is more surprising is that American Roman Catholic intellectuals, and the hierarchy as well, nearly always puzzled and sometimes defensive about High Church Anglicans like Cram, accepted Cram's leadership enthusiastically. A dean of the Catholic University of America, for example, once admitted in a letter to Cram that though he was an Episcopalian, no one had ever presented Catholic sacramental philosophy "so clearly and so cogently" as did Cram in a paper he gave on the subject.[7] Bishop Ryan, the Rector of Catholic University of America, once allowed Cram's publishers to print a letter of his about one of Cram's books in a promotional brochure.[8] Even in England, Chesterton and Belloc were glad enough of Cram's support, and Cram's *The Catholic Church and Art* (with both *Imprimatur* and *Nihil Obstat*, though Cram scarcely obscured his Anglicanism in his text) followed Chesterton's *The Catholic Church and Conversion* in 1930 in Belloc's Calvert Series. Belloc called Cram's book a "powerful essay"—"more definite and critical than I can remember to have seen elsewhere."[9] The *San Francisco Monitor*, the official organ of the Roman Catholic Archdiocese, to cite another instance, after lamenting that Cram was not a Roman Catholic—when he would convert (he never did) exercised as many people in this country as did the same question with respect to Chesterton (who did) in England—nevertheless insisted that Cram was "one of the great men of our time; a leader, almost a prophet," whose "Ordeal By Beauty" in *Convictions and Controversies* included some "of the most remarkable passages in all literature"![10] Astonishingly, no Roman Catholic in America ever exerted Cram's influence over the American Catholic Church his refusal to adhere to embarrassed so greatly.

Nor was Cram less well received in more strictly scholarly circles. A seminar on his writings was held in his lifetime at Holy Cross College.[11] And the author of *Impressions of Japanese Architecture*, who succeeded to a degree, incidentally, in carrying out the difficult commission of designing a convincing but not imitative Japanese garden court for the Museum of Fine Arts in Boston, was regularly appointed by the Museum trustees to the Visiting Committee of the Museum's Department of Asiatic Art. The author of *Ruined Abbeys of Great Britain* was invited as well to give the annual address in 1907 to the Royal Society of British Architects: Cram always enjoyed a transatlantic reputation. There were, of course, honorary doctorates, from Yale, Princeton, Williams, Rollins and

Notre Dame. Cram was also honorary Phi Beta Kappa at Harvard, where he gave the oration in 1921. And during his lifetime he was elected a fellow of a score of learned societies—including The Royal Society of Arts and the American Academy of Arts and Sciences—in the case of the last at the same time, interestingly, as Edna St. Vincent Millay and Carl Sandburg.[12] He was a member, of course, of a great many more. It was Cram who wrote the article on "American Architecture" in the twelfth edition of the *Encyclopaedia Britannica*.[13] He was also Henry Adams' literary heir in the matter of *Mont St. Michel and Chartres*, the copyright of which he presented to the American Institute of Architects. He wrote the preface to Adams' book, and gave the first of the Institute's Henry Adams Lectures at City Art Museum in St. Louis in 1934. Nor was his appointment to head the School of Architecture at M.I.T. in any sense an honorary affair: the president of "Tech" made it plain that he looked to Cram "to guide the school into a position of greater prestige and power."[14] But Cram's real measure as a scholar is perhaps best taken in his private correspondence with other scholars. Bernard Berenson, for instance, wrote Cram in a letter of 1941 that: "It's a real happiness to know that after at least fifty-six years of acquaintance we can understand each other better than ever."[15] Professor George Coffman, then Secretary of the Committee on Medieval Latin Studies at the American Council of Learned Societies, wrote to a mutual friend after Cram's death that "of the small choice group who talked and dreamed of the Medieval Academy [of America] before others became associated with us, [Cram] is most nearly irreplaceable." Concluded Coffman: "among the scholars and interpreters of the Middle Ages [Cram] was the artist and creator."[16] Professor E. K. Rand of Harvard thought hardly less of Cram, and in 1938 he wrote a moving appeal to Cram, who had thought to resign at age seventy-five, pointing out that "the Academy cannot give up your presence.... Please say 'yes' if you possibly can."[17] Nor was Cram as scholar only theologian and medievalist. He was historian and philosopher as well, and earned high praise from Brooks Adams, for example, who wrote to Cram in 1914 of one of Cram's more novel ideas that "... I incline to think that your theory of periods has a pretty sound historical basis, though it is new to me."[18] Cram's standing as a philosopher—he was often called "the Savant of Sudbury"—seems also to have been secure enough. Dr. Herman Radin, writing in *The Medical Pickwick* (one never knows where Cram will turn up), called Cram "the leading 'humanist' in America" in 1918.[19] Perhaps even more surprisingly, Professor Albert Jay Nock, whose field was American History and Politics, though he was perhaps best known for his translations and commentaries (with C. R. Wilson) on Rabelais, as well as for his numerous articles in the *Atlantic* and *The New Republic*, once wrote to Cram:

> ... my debt to you is greater than I owe to any other man or school. I have been five years trying to undermine the positions you took in your essay in man's place in Nature; with no success. They appear to be impregnable; and a study of their

correlations and implications has given me a philosophical position from which I have been able to account satisfactorily for all the phenomena of the subject which I had found completely puzzling.... You may judge from this how profound is the sense of obligation I have for you. Your professional reputation is so great that I believe it has overshadowed your claims as a philosopher. In a book I am preparing to write . . . I shall set forth your views at full length, if I live to finish the work, and be *ad hoc* your exposition. I re-read your autobiography, your *Convictions* and your *End of Democracy* twice a year, with ever-growing admiration for their quality.[20]

Insofar as his social theory verged on the political, as it often did, Cram's "notices" were naturally more mixed. When one of his most earnest causes was taken up by Franklin Roosevelt in the land subsistence homestead program this involved Cram in vigorous public argument. But even in this area he did not lack accolades: an official of the program in Minnesota wrote him in 1934 that a recent article Cram had written on the homestead plan was "the best that has been done on the subject."[21] Others of Cram's causes were more controversial. He labored strenuously to get this country into the First World War on the Allied side, and his stand earned public rebukes that ranged from "disgusting" to "jackass".[22] He also supported Al Smith strenuously—even to serving as Chairman of the Calvert Association Against Racial and Religious Bigotry that sponsored the series of controversial seminars on the subject at Harvard and at Columbia, one effect of which was Cram's inclusion in the "Who's Who" Issue of *The American Hebrew* as a friend of the Jewish people.[23] Finally, of course, Cram caused something of a sensation by later supporting Franklin Roosevelt. Under the heading "Pro-Cram" and "Anti-Cram," the *Boston Herald* printed five columns of letters in response to Cram's announcement. Elsewhere, R. M. Washburn remarked acidly that Cram had "now broken out in a new rash: He will vote for Franklin. Even worse than all this, Ralph is proud of it, and openly."[24] Cram, of course, thrived on it all. No doubt he thought it a compliment when one academic protested that a paper of his was "terrifically strong medicine" and admitted that "personally I could not have administered this dose."[25] And it certainly was a compliment when one of his editors, T. R. Shields of *The Educational Review*, allowed that he had not been so "stimulated" in years as by one of Cram's articles: "it is good for all of us," he wrote Cram, "to be made to think."[26] Only once did Cram show annoyance: when he had been interpreted as supporting Sir Arthur Conan Doyle's stand on Spiritualism in the preface Cram wrote for a British book, Frederick Bligh Bond's *Hill of Vision*. "On the contrary," retorted Cram, "I tried to controvert it. . . . Evidently, I don't express myself very well!"[27]

Usually, however, no one found any difficulty in discovering Cram's views. And whether pro or con, both his writings and lectures were taken very seriously. Their sheer quantity, of course, is astounding. His commencement addresses alone—which ranged from Yale (twice) to State University of Nebraska and Rice Institute in Texas—would make a good-sized book.[28] In the six years between 1930 and 1936, for instance, he wrote (in addition to four books) at least twenty-six articles, nine for professional journals, four for religious journals, six appeared in *American Mercury*, four in *American Review*, two in the *Atlantic Monthly* and one in *Time*. Even more startlingly, he wrote eight of his books in the nine years between 1914 and 1922—nearly one a year. Nor was he only to be found midst friends: that he should have corresponded with H. L. Mencken and been published so frequently by Paul Palmer in *American Mercury* is significant. His publishers, moreover, included Scribners, Macmillan, McGraw-Hill and Little Brown, and several of his books lasted through three or more editions.

It was difficult then (as it is now) to separate his popular, scholarly and more nearly polemical writings. But one book, particularly, which could fall under any of these rubrics, *Heart of Europe*, prompted a British critic to the perceptions in *The Times Literary Supplement* that are reproduced here on the prefatory page of opinions. The matter of Cram as a stylist, incidentally, also came up in this review, and no critic, I think, was ever more discerning than the *Times* critic when he described Cram's prose as "poured out in a headlong but often moving eloquence."[29] Here is an example having to do with Germany in the First World War, and more particularly of the bombardment of Rheims.

> ... And now a thing calling itself the highest civilization in Europe, with the name of God in its mouth, again sweeps the already well-swept land. In defiance of Peace Palaces and Conferences: ... the old arena of Europe flames as at Armageddon, while those things too sacred for pillage and destruction by the armies and the commanders of five centuries are given over to annihilation in order that the peril of the Slav may not menace the treasured civilization of the West, whose vestiges even now are blazing pyres, or cinders and ashes!

In the same work, though, and the *Times* critic quoted this, Cram's creative erudition sparkles in his analysis of early Gothic building. He thought it was characterized by "cohesion, economy and character."

> The first means the synthetic knitting of everything together, and the giving it dynamic power to develop from within outward; it means making structure absolutely central and comprehensive; but also beautiful; ornament, decoration, remaining something added to it, something of the *bene esse* though not of the *esse*; deriving from it in every instance, but not necessary to its perfection. The second is the reducing of mass to its logical and structural (and also optical) minimum, bringing into play the forces of accommodation, balance, and active, as opposed to passive, resistance. The third is the hardest to describe or determine, and probably can only be perceived through comparison. It is the differentiation in quality, the determination of personality, and it is hardly to be defined, though it is instantly perceived. In the Abbaye aux Hommes, or Cérisy, or St. Georges de Bocherville, we find

42. Sweet Briar College, Sweet Briar, Virginia

43. Wheaton College Chapel, Norton, Massachusetts

45. Central Congregational Church, Honolulu, Hawaii

47. Phillips Exeter Academy Administration Building, Exeter, New Hampshire

48. Williams College Library, Williamstown, Massachusetts

49. Cram's Japanese work, though not extensive, is important. For he was an authority on Japanese architecture, about which he wrote a much-admired book. He knew both Ernest Fenollosa and Okura Kakuzo of the Museum of Fine Arts in Boston very well, served on the Japanese Department's Visiting Committee and designed the Museum's Japanese Garden Court. Few remember, however, that this interest derived from his visit to Japan in 1899 and his design of that year for the Tokyo Parliament Buildings. Though the project fell victim to a subsequent change of governments, it was the occasion for one of Goodhue's most exquisite renderings, reproduced above from Cram's memoirs.

40. Choir, St. Vincent's Church, Los Angeles, California. **50.** Rollins College Chapel, Winter Park, Florida. **51.** Houston Public Library, Houston, Texas.

73–74. Where he judged it appropriate Cram no more hesitated to design a modernist Federal Building in Boston (right) in 1928 than he had in 1894 to design a Shingle Style suburban house (left) in Williamstown. The skyscraper, however, was a great disappointment. He discovered too late that the government intended only that he should "apply an exterior" to their design. Outraged, Cram noted in his memoirs that it was fatal to allow "the engineer to determine the organic form and then [call] on the architect to perform his window-dressing. . . ."

great majesty and beauty, many elements that are distinctive of true Gothic work and persist through its entire course, but none of these buildings is actually Gothic. In St. Germer de Fly, however, and in Sens and Noyan, while there seems at first little differentiation from the others, the Gothic spirit has found itself and is already working rapidly toward its consummation.[30]

When he was not theologian, philosopher, humanist, medievalist, historian, polemicist or social theorist—and in each both theorist and practitioner—Cram was still more things, though less importantly. The first Chairman of the Boston City Planning board, his proposals ranged from the fantastic (and beautiful) idea of an island in the Charles River to further enlarge the riverfront recreation areas and to provide for a new opera house (an idea revived in some measure by the Boston Arts Center plan of a few years ago) to completely obliterating all the "three-decker" districts in the city in favor of small single-family cottages of the sort he had seen and much liked around Tucson. (He went as often to the Southwest, which he loved, interestingly, as to Europe.) He was too, in his spare time, though indifferently, a poet, dramatist and lyricist. And even in these avocations, at the extreme periphery of his life, he earned attentions many might covet. Fred Bullard once did Cram's best-known song—"Nottingham Hunt"—at one of Bullard's Symphony Hall concerts, and in her younger years Rose Standish Nichols delighted in Cram's and Bullard's music at her famous Mt. Vernon Street "evenings."[31] These activities naturally figured most importantly in Cram's early Bohemian period in the 1890's—when he and Bullard and Bliss Carman, Bertram Goodhue, Thomas Meteyard, Herbert Small, Herbert Copeland, Daniel Updike, Fred Holland Day, Alice Brown, Bruce Rogers, Louise Imogen Guiney and Richard Hovey—all of whom became more or less famous for something in later life—joined forces in two rather notorious clubs, the Pewter Mugs and the Visionists. Their literary exploits (undertaken with more sober spirits like Charles Eliot Norton, Ernest Fenollosa, Bernard Berenson and Stephen Crane) included the now rather celebrated *Knight Errant*.[32] But all more or less carried over as time permitted into Cram's later life as well. Indeed, Cram's great dramatic success was the evidently quite gorgeous pageant he staged in 1916 for M.I.T. to mark the opening of the Cambridge campus. A letter has survived in the Library's collections to Cram from H. T. Parker, the legendary *Transcript* critic, in which Parker assured Cram that it was far better than any Oxford pageant—that, in fact, "neither in America or abroad have I yet seen one comparable with it."[33] The reader will perhaps now understand why even his eulogists found Cram an incredible figure, who they concluded could hardly have spent too much time at his drafting board, and why it is to some extent an unenviable task for me now to have to assert as well that he was a very hardworking and even a great architect. George H. Allen may have been right to conclude, in an article in 1931[34] for *Architectural Record*: "Ralph Adams Cram is a phenomenon."

More specifically, for all of his diverse activities were only the innumerable refractions of a philosophical unity of purpose,[35] Cram was among American architects in this century the first and perhaps the chief example of the sort of thing the *Harvard Magazine* has just recently remarked upon today in the American scientific community. Cram was in his own time one of the "stars" (today one might cite Margaret Mead, B. F. Skinner or Benjamin Spock) who, although leaders in their fields, are as well known for their involvement in social issues as for their professional work, who consistently make headlines and who have thus a large part in shaping Americans' attitudes in certain fields. Significantly, Mr. Goodell, the M.I.T. student whose Ph.D. dissertation, "The Visible Scientists," was the occasion for this recent report, concluded that though such "stars" invariably have established quite firm reputations within their own disciplines, they are not always popular among their colleagues. And in Cram's case, certainly, the astonishing success he enjoyed in and beyond architecture at the very least persuaded many that very little of Cram's work could be his own. His architectural reputation declined all the more quickly, therefore, after his death, because many of his peers—some, no doubt, out of jealousy, others more sincerely—denied him any substantial architectural accomplishment in the first place. And though his other accomplishments (no one doubted he wrote his own books) were not so easily dismissed, their sum only tended to confuse, and to make Cram an incredible figure. No one was ever very sure if he was the American Ruskin or the American Pugin, or both.

This is also probably the reason that our rediscovery of Cram, firstly, has been rather "piecemeal," in the form, as it were, of "extracts" of various sorts; and, secondly, has not begun with his architecture, though he is generally still best known as an architect. In 1966, for instance, the editors of Dover Press persuaded themselves that Cram's *Impressions of Japanese Architecture* was a "minor classic," and this of all books was thus the first of Cram's to be reissued in paperback. In 1970, in my senior year at Harvard, when I was so amazed in the course of researching rather a routine paper on Cram at how cavalierly this major figure had been treated that I amazed myself by working up a monograph that was published in the spring of 1971 (and subsequently in 1972 by the Tribune Publishing Company under the title of *The Gothic Churches of Dorchester*), I concentrated on Cram's architectural theory. Only in the companion volume did I begin to deal with his actual practice, and only peripherally with his philosophy of art. It was not until my *Church Building in Boston* of last year that I began really to focus on Cram as a designer, a factor that will also I think be emphasized in the doctoral dissertation on Cram's early churches now being completed at the University of North Carolina at Chapel Hill by Ann Miner Daniel. In the meantime, however, not only the "Japanese" Cram, but the social theorist and the "literary" Cram have already surfaced. In 1972, Professor Robert Muccigrosso at Brooklyn College (intrigued by the fact that though "leading students of American thought invariably have classified Cram as a conservative," he had been, "unlike other conservatives of the 1930's, most sympathetic to Roosevelt") published an article in the Fordham University Quarterly in which he argued that "Cram was considerably more than a twentieth century 'nay-sayer'"—that, in fact, "when irresponsible conservatism probably reached its zenith" in the 30's, Cram, on the other hand, had been able to "forge in the crucible of the Depression a synthesis between his medievalism and the needs of his own society" that however dubious or distasteful in some ways, nonetheless in Muccigrosso's view can be said to "represent and expand upon the possibilities of the conservative imagination." Just after Muccigrosso's article, moreover, a short story by Cram turned up in a new anthology of English and American literature, presumably entirely on its literary merits, and in company with no less than Dickens, de Maupassant and Henry James. And just recently an assistant professor of religion at Miami University, Oxford, Ohio, Peter Williams, has attempted a paper that deals largely with Charles Eliot Norton, Henry Adams and Ralph Adams Cram.[36] Here, then, is the Japanese scholar, the architectural theorist, the social theorist, the writer and the philosopher—rising seemingly at random and quite separately to the surface—and significantly in advance of the architect. His posterity, not unnaturally, is shying away from the complete Cram, and is shaping him much the same way his contemporaries did, and for almost the same reasons. And his reputation as a designer having always been suspect, and having therefore declined the more quickly, as the relative notice taken of his death in the architectural and popular press shows, it has been the last to revive.

It is true that one or two scholars, even so early as in the 50's, have broken loose to notice Cram's architecture. Walter Taylor, writing in 1952 in Talbot Hamlin's *Forms and Functions of Twentieth Century Architecture*, conceded that Cram's Gothic school, characterized by "deep conviction, truth to structure, and exquisite detail," at times produced "monuments of superb quality," and in fact that in his view Cram's Gothic movement "provided the intellectual background" for the "organic architecture" of the 50's.[37] Nor, in the 1955 edition of *Sticks and Stones*, did Lewis Mumford modify his conclusion of 1924 that the "triumphs have been genuine" in Cram's church and collegiate work.[38] But it is only very recently that we have begun really to recover some sense of Cram himself as an architect. In 1974, Gerald Allen, writing enough in advance of a definitive scholarship to be misled once or twice, nonetheless got so carried away by one of Cram's New York churches as to describe it as "boldly original" —in an article in *Architectural Record* significantly subtitled: "some practical lessons for building in *today's* cities [my italics] by Ralph Adams Cram and Bertram Grosvenor Goodhue"![39] And just this fall, an architect, Jay Sadler, in his new book on the Gothic Revival for the New York Graphic Society, remarks wonderingly on "Cram's almost uncanny ability to find the most visually satisfying solution to every problem."[40]

It is very likely, however, that this last stage of our recovery of Cram's achievement, having to do with his architecture, will prove the most difficult. For though it is of crucial importance that we understand that all Cram's activities coalesced in a very organic way, and that we must not, therefore, fall into the trap of continuing to abstract only one or two at a time for discussion, and thus never discover the philosophical unity of the whole, architectural historians no less than social or religious historians will necessarily be forced to run this danger. And it will be most dangerous in this case, because the integrity of Cram's architecture will be hard to establish without reference to his philosophy of art and his architectural theory. And in both cases some rude shocks await us; shocks that probably explain why, for instance, the pattern I have underlined here, in his obituaries as elsewhere, has just now again been repeated in the 1975 *Britannica*, where though Cram is among the very few American architects given a full-fledged half-column-length biographical entry under his name, his architecture is under that heading elsewhere dismissed in a sentence or two. The trauma will be subtle, moreover, and lies in the fact that we invariably rehabilitate our ancestors in strict chronological order. Consequently, though we are prepared to understand Cram's struggle with Modernism—else we would not be discovering Victorian architecture so enthusiastically—we have not yet perhaps understood either the effect of this struggle on art historical scholarship on Cram in the recent past, or the effect Cram's much less well known combat with Victorian architecture is likely to have on our own scholarship today. As an architect, Cram may well prove more difficult to rehabilitate than he has been to rediscover.

II. *THEORY*

From the beginning of his career, as the art critic of the *Boston Transcript* and after 1889 as a practicing architect, and throughout his long life he held tenaciously to this view, Cram condemned outright by far the largest part of American architecture after 1820. Richardson and McKim were his chief American heroes: with very few exceptions the rest either outraged or, worse, bored him. Before Richardson he thought American architecture "more savage, more corrupt, more revolting in all its details than ever had been recorded . . .": a statement he admitted was "strong"—but he insisted he "would maintain it under persecution."[41] And in his maturity, in 1914, though he thought it better, he still asserted that when criticizing Modernism one had to remember that "on the other hand, the astute archaeology of some of our *best* modern work whether Classic or Gothic is stupefying and leads nowhere"![42] American architecture, he announced in the same year, was to a large extent still "bound hand and foot to a traditionalism that is Byzantine in its rigidity and mounts often to the level of an historic superstition."[43] None of his now better known modernist contemporaries savaged "traditionalism" any the worse than did Cram.

Even in the case of Richardson, whose disciple Cram was as a young man in the 1880's, Cram made it clear that it was Richardson's *handling* of Trinity Church, not his Romanesque, which he admired, and Cram always insisted that Richardson would be remembered for the creative rebirth of American architecture his vitality precipitated rather than for his stylistic propensities. Trinity, Cram held, and he said as much of McKim's Copley Square Library, possessed "force and majesty and authority": it was, he claimed a "solid, consistent and beautiful" episode midst "all the ridiculous and ugly effigies" of his youth.[44] But through Henry Vaughan, Cram early found more pertinent heroes in the English Gothicists—notably Pierson, Sedding and Bodley—and in John Ruskin.[45] Thus in the earliest writings the Library possesses of Cram's—his 1885 journal—he was already ruminating as a young man of twenty-two on the fact that American Gothicists "not only copy the deficiencies as well as the beauties [of medieval gothic], but they make modern necessities conform to Gothic forms. It does not seem," wrote Cram, "as though such servile copying is true art."[46] It was the same point he would make over and over again for the next half century in his torrent of books, articles and lectures. It was the background, for example, for his contention that Scott's Liverpool Cathedral was *the* modern Gothic masterpiece: it was, wrote Cram, "as far removed from precedent as possible,"[47] which is not the reason most of us would expect Cram to have given for liking a church. It was also the reason for his (to us) astonishing admonition to his generation that "above all else, let us remember this . . . we are building for now . . . it is art, not archaeology that drives us. . . ."[48] Though he believed that "all the art of every time is founded on some specific art in the past," he asserted vigorously that "if it remains in bondage to this older art, if it wanders in the twilight of precedent or, in fear and trembling, chains itself to the rock of archaeology, then again it ceases to be art—ceases? no; it has never even begun; it is only a dreary mocking of a shattered idol, a futile picture puzzle to beguile a tedious day."[49] The curious thing, of course, is that Cram was actually forever battling against what most critics have subsequently concluded he stood for!

But the key to an understanding of why Cram could say these things lies in the fact that he had discerned murder and not exhaustion in the abrupt termination at the time of the Reformation of Gothic architecture; for he built his rationale on the controversial premise that Montgomery Schuyler associated himself with in his lengthy discussion of Cram and Goodhue's work in *Architectural Record* in 1911: that "*the Gothic principle is the very principle of progress, and faithfully applied to modern conditions would result in an architecture as unlike in form* [*but*] *as kindred in spirit to the medieval building in which thus far it has found its most triumphant expression.*"[50] Accordingly, Cram could not understand why American Gothicists, instead of trying to take up the 16th century threads and *logically develop them through a creative scholarship*, chose not to try to weave anew so that they might through a study of Gothic principles further develop and refine this architecture to the original service of their own time, but chose instead to study to death, as it were, the old medieval forms, as if they were all the life Gothic could ever have. The question he posed had thus to do more than anything with *what was and what was not Gothic*. And his primary contention was that it was organism, not form, that should be studied, "principles . . . not moldings," and that the reverse having become fashionable the substance of Gothic architecture, the development of the Gothic organism into new forms as these were needed for a heightened functional pertinence, was always lacking. One saw, instead, Cram thought, either a perverse scholarship in dead forms, un-Gothic because such a copybook Gothic had no structural authority or artistic integrity; or a perverse spontaneity in new forms, un-Gothic because they did not arise from Gothic principles of design and construction, but, rather, more often than not repudiated them. The former was a case, Cram thought, of *careful reproduction*: the latter of *careless reminiscence*. Ralph Adams Cram, Charles Maginnis would later assert, "pleaded without ceasing for an honest architecture of blood and muscle for the scenic mimicry of historic form."[51]

Nor was this only verbal camouflage. No more startling illustration of Cram's emphasis on Gothic principles rather than on Gothic forms is extant than his discussion of construction in his very first editorial in *Christian Art*, in 1907, where Cram argued strongly for the study of the frank use of steel and reinforced concrete in *Gothic* church construction; noting that it would be wrong to suggest Gothic could not honestly use this new "structural expedient, equally novel and hitherto unthought of," precisely because "the essence of Gothic lies not in the established forms . . . but in the acceptance of principles." Lest this seem outrageous, it may be pertinent to cite here a definition of style by Viollet-le-Duc that Cram must have known: "Style," he said, "is the consequence of a principle methodically followed." Cram frankly admitted that he did not know what "a master mason of the great Middle Ages" would have done "with steel and [reinforced] concrete ready to hand" or how he would have "gone to work to evolve a logical and a beautiful and a significant result from these materials," but, Cram insisted, "we know he would have done it" and, moreover, "we know also that his masterly sense of reason and logic would have forbidden him to build up his steel frame and fashion his vaults and floors of reinforced concrete, and then hide them by inoperative arches, piers and buttresses of decorative stone in the silly hope that so he might fool the public into thinking they possessed a consistent work of art."[52]

PLEASE FOLD OUT

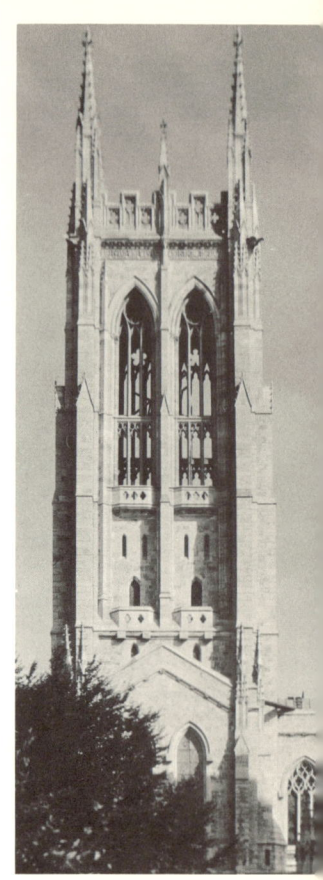

8.   11.   1

9.   12.

10.   13.

1.

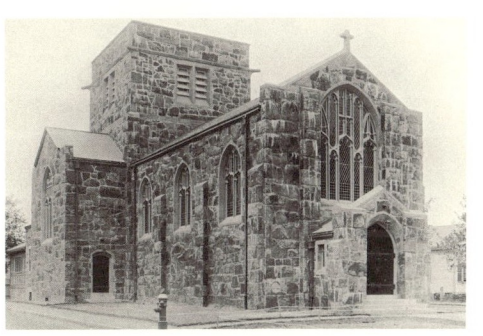

2.

4.

3.

5.

6.

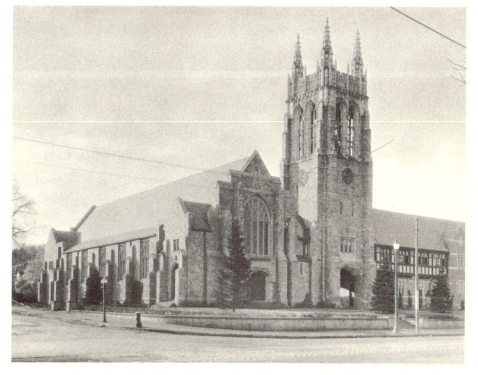

7.

GOTHIC WORK

1. All Saints' Church, Ashmont, Dorchester, Boston, Massachusetts
2. Church of Our Saviour, Middleboro, Massachusetts
3. St. Stephen's Church, Cohasset, Massachusetts
4. St. Thomas' Church, Fifth Avenue, New York City
5. St. Mary's Church, Redford, Detroit, Michigan
6. Emmanuel Church, Newport, Rhode Island
7. First Unitarian Church, Newton, Massachusetts
8. Euclid Avenue Presbyterian Church, Cleveland, Ohio
9. Chapel, Holy Cross Monastery, West Park, New York
10. All Saints' Church, Peterborough, New Hampshire
11. Calvary Church, Pittsburgh, Pennsylvania
12. House of Good Hope Presbyterian Church, St. Paul, Minnesota
13. St. Paul's Church, Yonkers, New York
14. Swedenborgian Church, Bryn Athyn, Pennsylvania
15. St. Paul's Church, Winston-Salem, North Carolina
16. Conventual Church of St. Mary and St. John, Cambridge, Massachusetts
17. East Liberty Presbyterian Church, Pittsburgh, Pennsylvania
18. Second Presbyterian Church, Lexington, Kentucky
19. Mercersburg Academy Chapel, Mercersburg, Pennsylvania
20. Princeton University Graduate College, Princeton, New Jersey
21. Ellingwood Mortuary Chapel, Nahant, Massachusetts
22. Atwood House, East Gloucester, Massachusetts
23. Harris Chapel, Rydal, Georgia
24. Post Headquarters, United States Military Academy, West Point, New York
25. St. James' Church, Lake Delaware, New York
26. Church of The Ascension, Montgomery, Alabama
27. The Cathedral Church of St. John The Divine, New York City. (Cram's master plan. The choir as originally built and four of the five chevet chapels are not by Cram. Not visible in this perspective are Cram's Bishop's House, Deanery and Synod House.)
28. St. Elizabeth's Chapel, Cram Estate, Sudbury, Massachusetts
29. Church of The Holy Rosary, Pittsburgh, Pennsylvania
30. Watkins House, Winona, Illinois
31. Desloge Hospital Chapel, St. Louis, Missouri
32. St. Mary's Church, Walkerville, Ontario, Canada
33. St. George's School Chapel, Newport, Rhode Island

27.

28.

30.

32.

29.

31.

33.

17.
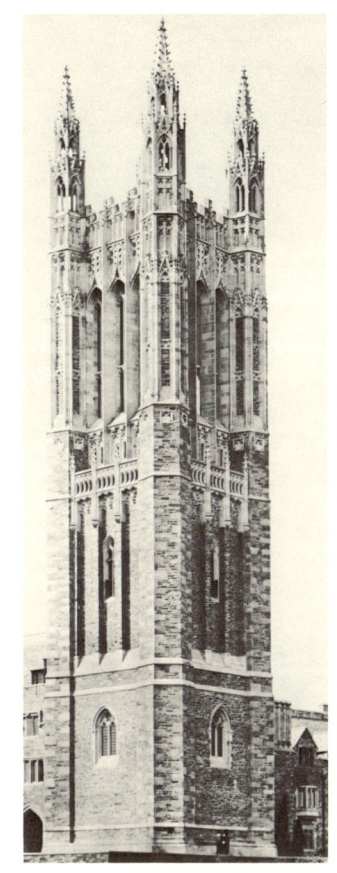
20.

24.

18.

21.

25.
19.

22.

23.
26.

The principle was in this case easier for Cram to arrive at than the application. Though he experimented repeatedly with concrete in his churches—even designing the home office of the Economy Concrete Company (with figure sculpture in that material modeled by Lee Lawrie)—he was so perennially disappointed by its inadequacies that he never explored the reverse of N. F. Cachemaille-Day's later and fascinating thesis that "the natural development of reinforced concrete construction for churches leads one back to the point where Gothic architecture in England left off . . . namely late perpendicular architecture."[53] This was unfortunate, for the fundamental premise of Cram's earliest work was precisely that though the Classic and Romanesque styles were not proper to the late 19th century because they were "the expression of conditions that are utterly unlike those that now obtain," Gothic was proper because its development had been artificially aborted by the Reformation and was only moribund and thus susceptible to a new development.[54] And this doctrine of development is particularly vital to any discussion of Cram, because it differentiates Cram importantly from Pugin, as well as from the first generation of American Gothicists Richardson had overwhelmed so decisively. For Pugin asserted that "Christian architecture had gone its length" by the Reformation and that "it must necessarily have destroyed itself thereafter."[55] Cram, on the other hand, ever held that beautiful as were the results of the religious builders of the 15th century, they themselves had almost infinite capacity for still nobler works," but that this capacity was never realized because by the early 16th century "churches were no longer built, but destroyed instead."[56] From which Cram deduced that modern Gothicists should "go back to the 16th century not to endeavor to build churches that shall pretend to have been built in that century,"[57] but, rather, in order that modern Gothicists might then "work steadily and seriously towards something more consistent with our temper and the times in which we live."[58] This development, he was sure, would soon shed "the close resemblance to its model that is at first inevitable."[59]

Accordingly, Cram never ceased experimenting with new ideas.[60] Indeed, he happily made use of a multitude of very modern techniques and materials in his work, but frankly, and not disguised as stone or wood or marble, and only when something modern was an improvement on medieval practice. He was pleased indeed to be able to banish the medieval fire hazard of wooden roofs above vaults, for instance, and cheerfully reported in his memoirs that he had supported the roof of St. John The Divine with great steel trusses encased in concrete. The piers and vaults below, however, are what they seem—entirely self-supporting masonry. Had these been something else they would have looked like something else. At his Calvary Church in Detroit Cram noted in the guidebook that the floors were reinforced concrete, as in a similar description of his House of Good Hope Presbyterian Church in St. Paul, Minnesota, he noted that reinforced concrete slabs formed the aisle roofs. There is also machine carving in wood in his churches. Cram knew that nothing could be counted upon to deaden any man's artistry more quickly than the need to endlessly repeat running miles of moldings and he was thus happy to be able to free him from that tedium in order that he might have sufficient time and spirit to develop creatively the lavish figure sculpture Cram wanted him to concentrate on. Then, too, the Cram office is repeatedly singled out in Wallace Sabine's papers as having stimulated the greater part of his pioneering research into architectural acoustics. In this connection, too, it was Cram's improbable modern Gothic thesis that a Gothic church could only be really Gothic if it was really modern, and solve every new as well as every perennial problem, that stimulated Wallace Sabine and Rafael Guastavino to their experiments with acoustical tiles. Cram wanted real Gothic vaults, and often high ones, but he wanted also to answer the new need of his own time for the liturgy to be clearly heard. Thus Guastavino and Sabine collaborated on this problem, and it was that collaboration which yielded what Guastavino called "the first patent on an acoustical ceramic tile," used at St. Thomas, New York, and that later led to their non-ceramic product, "akoustolith."[61]

Cram, of course, scoffed at his detractors' conclusion that his Gothic movement was "aiming to bring back in all its integrity both a dead civilization and its forms." He insisted that "such an idea would be far from the facts."[62] He knew well enough, as remarked once in an article, that "life in the Middle Ages was for the greater number of men, hard and in many ways unlovely . . . ,"[63] but though he found more virtues than most in the medieval period, he rebuked scathingly critics who misunderstood his thesis to mean that he would turn back the clock.

> Shall we rest there. Shall we restore a style, and a way of life, and a mode of thought? Shall we recreate an amorphous medievalism and live listlessly in that fool's paradise: On the contrary. When a man finds himself confronting a narrow stream, with no bridge in sight, does he leap convulsively on the very brink and then project himself into space? If he does he is very apt to fail of his immediate object, which is to get across. No, he retraces his steps, gains his running start, and clears the obstacle at a bound. This is what we architects are doing when we fall back on the great past for our inspiration; this is what, specifically, the Gothicists are particularly doing. We are getting our running start, we are retracing our steps to the great Christian Middle Ages, not that there we may remain, but that we may achieve an adequate point of departure; *what follows must take care of itself.* (my italics)[64]

His was the reformer's perennial recourse. Historians have perhaps emphasized too much the manner of Cram's retracing of steps, and virtually never considered whether or not he got his running start, much less leaped, or gained the other shore.

Having early announced that "absolute beauty" amounted to "perfect adap-

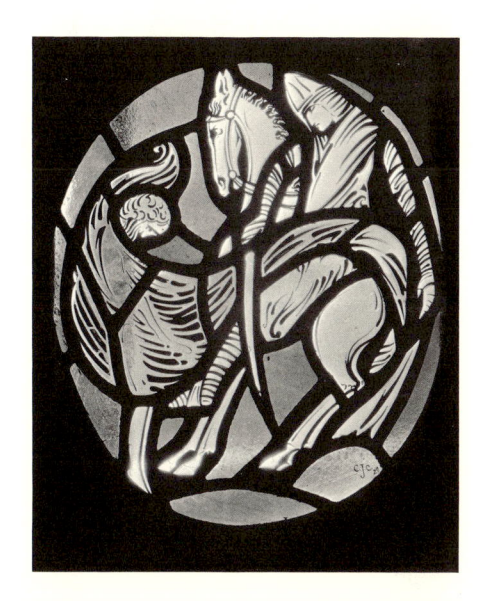

55–56–58. Cram insisted that everything, from hardware to vestments, and including music and ceremonial as well, should always be reticently integrated by the church building into an organic unity that expressed artistically not only the Catholic sacramental philosophy of matter and spirit but the corporate rather than individualistic convention of Catholic liturgy. Thus, although it sometimes took decades, Cram sought always to design everything in his churches, or to supervise the work of trusted artist-collaborators. These included Charles Connick (above, right, his St. Martin and The Beggar in Honolulu), John Angel (above, left, his St. Joan at St. John The Divine in New York) or Johannes Kirchmayer (above, his triptych at All Saints', Ashmont, in Boston).

52. First Presbyterian Church, Tacoma, Washington

53. Doheny Library, University of Southern California, Los Angeles, California

54. Rice Institute Administration Building, Houston, Texas

tion to form,"[65] and that, in fact, it was in large part precisely this quality in Gothic architecture that had drawn Cram so strongly to its modern development; and ready as Cram was to admit that "all the arts of the late nineteenth century were retrospective, archaeological . . ."; and that the artistic revival of that time had expressed itself "in an almost complete artificiality";[66] Cram consequently never failed to point out that "Modernism tried logically to correct this" and that it was therefore "a healthy sign" because it was only proper that the new "technological civilization . . . should show itself in an adequate art."[67] It would be "absurd," he thought, "to build a school of mechanical engineering or a chemistry library after the stylistic fashion of an Oxford College" or "a gymnasium like a medieval abbey"[68] and he heaped a good deal of abuse on the "Gothic" skyscrapers of his own day.[69] Movie houses, airplane hangars, department stores, skyscrapers—these, he thought, were as inevitably modernist as an automobile. Imagine, he challenged, a "Byzantine motor car"![70] Nor did he deny that Modernism could be beautiful. "There is a certain and undeniable beauty," he admitted, "in the true modern style."[71] And he cited a "well designed motor car," or an airplane of similar quality as a case in point—either, he thought was "a beautiful thing."[72] He also delighted in modernist "shop fronts and display windows and—in France—in jewelry, decorative details and small sculpture,"[73] and was particularly fascinated with photography; a new "art" he called it, and admired much of it.[74] Not surprisingly, given his fascination in terms of design with mass and set-back, he cited both the Nebraska State Capitol and the Empire State Building as "monuments of intelligent architecture . . . true modernism."[75] Though he disliked most skyscrapers, he thought it was in these towering new forms that American architecture had nonetheless "achieved its most vital and original results"[76] by 1922. He admitted freely that they fascinated him—because they were "couched in terms of new materials with no stylistic connotations whatever"—and complained bitterly that when at last he thought he had his chance at one, the Boston Federal Building, the government instead had only expected him to "apply an exterior."[77]

He liked, too, the new domestic architecture he saw around Tucson in the early 30's.[78] He was pleased at the increasing frankness in design, and conceded freely that to the extent that the modernist artist had destroyed "the stale and sterile formulae of Victorian art" it was certainly true that "we owe him much for this."[79] But a good deal of Modernism he didn't like at all. Typical was this headline in a St. Louis paper in 1934: "Architect Cram Flays 'Hellish' Modern Designs."[80] More soberly, believing as he did that there was "ground enough for revolt" from late Victorian art (he had been, after all, to his mind, one of the rebels), he allowed that "we cheer them on" when, for example, "Matisse in decent scorn and disgust paints his protest."[81] But though he thought the "rebels of that day were great people," he quickly concluded that all their "camp-followers" had learned was "the impulse of revolt,"[82] and cautioned that "we are no more bound thereafter to their following than we should have been to that of Marat or Robespierre because we had taken part in that affair of the Tennis Court."[83] Moreover, he warned, however necessary the destroyers, "the power that destroys can never under any circumstances rebuild,"[84] however brilliant its adherents. He greatly admired Louis Sullivan, whom he thought "a very great genius." He admitted Frank Lloyd Wright was a genius. But, cautioned Cram, he was a "less responsible genius."[85]

The crucial mistake of Modernism to Cram was "the assumption that there were no values existing other than the new ones...." For "however intimately [Modernism] might relate itself to the new technological society" it did not, Cram warned, relate at all to the church, and hardly at all to the school or the home.[86] Architecturally, he thought that just as it was absurd to build chemistry libraries in the form of medieval abbeys, so also was it "equally absurd and perfectly pointless and ungrammatical to couch a ... college chapel in the terms of a ... skyscraper."[87] It was, he thought, *unfunctional*. For he ever asserted that "a building must look like what it is, express visibly the energy that informs it, and declare its spiritual and intellectual lineage."[88] Moreover, he warned that *precisely because* modernist art was a legitimate expression of a technological and rampantly materialistic culture (where matter had usurped spirit rather than expressing it) the school, the home, and the church particularly, could only embrace it at great peril. The result, thought Cram, would be "fatal in its consequences"[89]—particularly because he saw Modernism as the latest issue of the "thoroughly secularized" art of the Renaissance. That, he believed, on one level, was "a good thing, and not to be rejected," since religious sense he knew had become "an attribute of only a minority" and as art was "a part of man's birthright" he always believed that it was "only fair that [this secularized art] should exist and be fostered in the secular sphere."[90] Naturally, though, he thought the Church would be mad to go over to it. He did admit that "past ages ... manifested their spirit through only one style that held for everything," but doubted that in the 20th century—an era of "change, when an era comes to its end, and another rises to take its place"—we possessed the "substantial unity, social, economic, political and religious," to evolve a single new modern style.[91] He wrote:

> ... I do not wish to be considered as one who would condemn modernist art *in toto*: it has a very useful place ..., it is yet the true expression of the technological, materialistic age in which we now find ourselves, and where it is used for the voicing of the manifestation of that type of civilization ... it is all right, it should be used; but when it is employed for the expression of traditional and unchangeable things, that is, the fundamental things (I always think of them as the home, the school and the church) which sometimes change in form or in accidents, but do not change in fundamental qualities; ... I think it is subject to condemnation.[92]

40. Baptistry, St. John The Divine, New York City

37. Chancel, All Saints' Church, Peterborough, New Hampshire

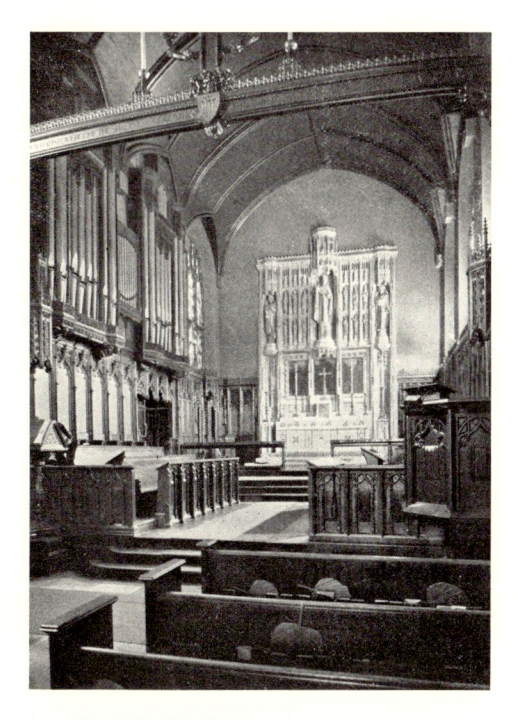

35. Chancel, All Saints', Ashmont, Boston, Massachusetts

36. Nave, Sacred Heart Church, Jersey City, New Jersey

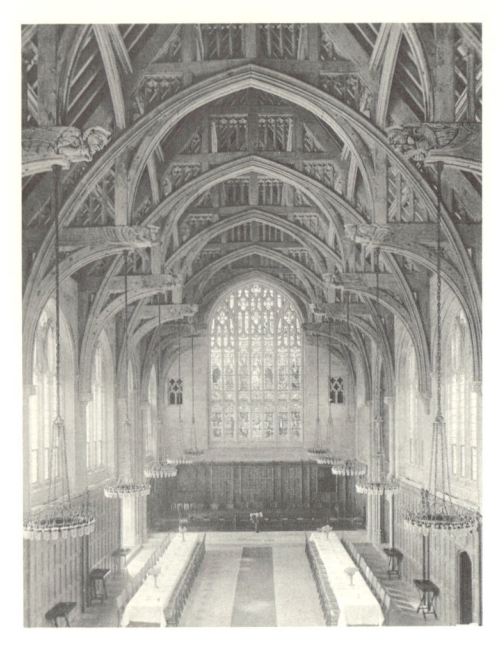

39. Graduate College Commons, Princeton University

34. Chancel, East Liberty Church, Pittsburgh, Pennsylvania

38. Chantry, St. Thomas' Church, New York City

40 A. Chapel, Conventual Church, Cambridge, Massachusetts

Cram did not ignore the new things. He welcomed some of them, accepted a great many more as inevitable and repudiated a good many too. He tried, in other words (never for a moment concealing his bias, for he was the preeminent artistic spokesman of Catholicism in America), to *discriminate*.

But consider, for instance, Cram's insistence, as early as in 1899, on "the prime necessity of a rigid honesty in church building,"[93] or his condemnation of "false construction [as] simply a lie told for reasons of penury or ostentation."[94] Study too his advice to fellow architects that "it costs no more to build a good church than a bad one; less in fact, for the trouble with many architects . . . is that they do not know how to stop when they get through. Good architecture . . . is primarily a matter of form, proportion, composition, well chosen materials and absolute honesty of construction."[95] Recall, as well, what he wrote in 1914:

> The steel frame is the *enfant terrible* of architecture, but like so many of the same genus it may grow up to be a serious-minded citizen and a good father. . . . If we can make it realize that it is a new force, not a substitute, we shall do well. When it contents itself in its own proper sphere . . . then it may be a good servant. Like all good servants it makes the worst possible master; and when it claims as its chiefest virtue that it enables us to reproduce the Baths of Caracalla, vaults and all, at half the price, or build a second Chartres Cathedral with no danger from thrusting arches, and with flying buttresses that may be content beautifully to exist, since they will have no other work to do, then it is time to call a halt. The foundation of good architecture is structural integrity, as the Pennsylvania Station in New York; if its columns merely hide the working steel within, if its vast vaults are plaster on steel frame and expanded metal then it is not architecture, it is scene painting.[96]

Now consider how this fundamental constituent of Cram's revival of church architecture in this country in the 1900–30 period has been disclosed to us—in, for instance, a large and well-received volume of 1962, entitled *Modern Church Architecture*. Necessarily an attempt to persuade us to give up our lingering fondness for pointed arches, was it even accurate to report that "the 1930's were the turning point in [an] exciting period of liberation from outworn cliches . . ." the constituents of which are described as follows: "the play of vault against buttress, the daring originality of thin walls and large openings . . . became in our time the dead weight of steel columns, plaster vaults painted to simulate stone, buttresses that buttressed nothing. . . . This miserable deception in a place where truth reigns supreme! An architect building a church must be sensitive to the ridiculous!"[97] It sounds very much, does it not, like the Cram of the 1890's savaging Victorian Gothic. Again, one sees Cram and his disciples standing for exactly what they repudiated.

Moreover, consider Cram's entire accomplishment. Remember, however curious his Gothic quest, that he achieved in his lifetime an astonishing popular success; that he shaped American church design in his own image for three decades; that he has left us not only his buildings but nearly two dozen books, the majority of which state his views on art and architecture at some length; that his designs were praised extravagantly by men of some professional distinction; that he was, for instance, one of only three or four living American architects to earn a full-fledged biographical notice in the 1922 *Britannica*. Consider again the type and content of his obituaries, and then consider the assertion of a present-day authority on church design, in the journal of the Guild for Religious Architecture, an affiliate of the American Institute of Architects, that in Cram's time, before 1924, religious architecture in America was so bad that " *'architectural merit' was almost non-existent.*"[98] This astounding assertion, made in all seriousness, perhaps illustrates to perfection why even by the time of his death, Cram was more interesting to the *Times* of London or to the *Baltimore Sun* than to the architectural press. Fundamentally, Cram has been increasingly a victim of what Margaret Henderson Floyd has called "the shadow of the Modern Movement, which has so colored art historical scholarship in this century."[99] Indeed, the root of the matter is that Cram had the audacity to pursue his Gothic quest into the 20th century, and with such an enormous success that he was able to offer a moderate "modernist" alternative, in church design particularly, that until his death in 1942 challenged all too effectively in at least one area the final victory his modernist contemporaries fought for with scarcely less fervor. Cram was among those, wrote Lewis Mumford (and Mumford concluded that Richardson was another), who "stood outside the currents of their time and kept their position."[100] Indeed, Cram's Century Club obituary emphasized this, remarking that Cram's

> . . . vivid vehemence was as stimulating as the proverbial intellectual cocktail. That the period of his greatest creative output coincided with the early beginnings of the modern movement . . . was only a fresh incentive to his prolific pen and pencil. Always a storm center, singularly provocative, unhesitatingly outspoken . . . there are few of his contemporaries who have not differed with him, even while admiring his courage and recognizing his scholarly defenses. Many have held that his Gothic was but the empty shell of a past for which there is no place in the world of today. But to him it was still the living force. . . . Each (to him) new revelation of architectural beauty . . . became a priceless discovery to be shared with a hungry public. . . ."[101]

And they were still hungry in the age of Franklin Roosevelt. The Depression bit hard into Cram's pocketbook—great churches (alas) are luxuries—but insofar as the public was concerned not at all into his prestige. In December of 1930, the editors of *Fortune*, in an article on Cram (who was then in his sixty-eighth year) noticed that "before the War the names of three great partnerships dominated any discussion of American architecture—McKim, Mead and White; Carrere and Hastings; and Cram, Goodhue and Ferguson. . . . Mr. Cram alone survives," the article continued, and even into "the age of steel and reinforced concrete."[102] And that the article should have appeared in *Fortune* in the first place will indicate that Cram's prestige was scarcely declining. Even his practice easily weathered the Great Depression. He designed and built the single most costly Gothic church of his life in the 30's—the East Liberty Church in Pittsburgh—and though it was nowhere near completed (then or now) in the last year of his life, and only a week before Pearl Harbor, he was able to walk the full length of potentially the largest cathedral in the world, *his* cathedral, after having again voted enthusiastically for Franklin Roosevelt—"the one supreme politician since Lincoln!"[103] No wonder he alike diverted and confused so many of his peers, and so infuriated the modernists that they were forced—almost in self-defense—to rewrite the history books.

Cram thus emerges as that most interesting and most complex of historical figures, inevitably misunderstood by his posterity because too many had a vested interest in doing so. Cram was a revolutionary whose revolution triumphed, but then withered and died when he died, and thus left his reputation hostage to his modernist opponents, who were not slow to take advantage of the scarcely credible extent of all his accomplishments, or of his declining reputation as a designer. Not unnaturally, moreover, the modernists saw in the demise of Cram's moderate Modernism after his death, the final proof of the inevitability of their own success. For as it turned out, without Cram, the church fell easily. Cram, like Cromwell in that his revolution could not survive without him, in the end seems more like Trotsky. It is easy to forget the revolutionary who fails. Who mourns the Mensheviks? Certainly not the Bolsheviks. And the modernists did not mourn Cram.

III. *PARTNERSHIP*

IF this revisionism was the more readily acceptable to the general public because of the seeming legendary quality of Cram, it was all the more persuasive to architects and scholars alike because of the controversial nature of Cram's relationship with his first designing partner, Bertram Grosvenor Goodhue. A genius in his own right to whom in Cram's lifetime those who doubted Cram spent much time at a drafting board naturally pointed, Goodhue, moreover, died just in time, in the sense that his last work, notably the Nebraska State Capitol, was sufficiently more modernist to allow his posterity to speculate as their biases dictated. Cram himself saw in the Nebraska Capitol a convincing Modernism, far closer to Cram's tastes than that of Louis Sullivan, but the modernists themselves, and not without reason, were quick to point to the likelihood (had Goodhue lived) of a defection scarcely less historic than Cardinal Newman's. And while they were undermining the integrity of explicit revivalism generally, they were thus easily able to explain away Cram's successes by ascribing them mostly to Goodhue, and then to rob them of any embarrassment by pointing to the fact that Goodhue seemed headed relentlessly towards Modernism at the time of his death.

But the theory that Goodhue was the firm's only or even chief designer, however apparently plausible, derived from nothing more than hearsay: and nothing but hearsay has ever been advanced in support of it. One has only to look at Cram's submission and Goodhue's—before they had met—to the 1887 St. John The Divine competition to see at once in what was presumably each man's best effort (and it is the only test we have of the sort) that Cram was at least in the beginning a vastly better designer than Goodhue. Cram's watercolors and sketches for the firm before Goodhue's advent, furthermore, demonstrate conclusively not only Cram's power of independent design but the fact that the firm's earliest work—including All Saints, Ashmont—was at the very least the result of a design concept of Cram's that Goodhue accepted. Nor did Goodhue's advent at once lift the firm's work up to any startling new excellence of design: Saint Paul's, Brockton—where the deep pier buttresses *midst the west window* (buttressing what?) disclose a habit of Goodhue's Cram had no use for—possesses perhaps the most illiterate and banal west front they ever attached their names to in a quarter century of partnership.

Goodhue's coming to the firm—as a draughtsman in 1889 and as junior partner in 1892—was, however, of crucial importance in two other ways. Firstly, Goodhue's pen-and-ink renderings surely sold as many clients as Cram's articles and books—for Bertram Goodhue was even by the mid-1890's a considerable artist and probably the best draughtsman in the country. Secondly, the firm's detail, rather wooden and uninspired at first, evolved quickly after Goodhue's arrival into the most astonishingly suave and exquisite Gothic work ever seen in this country. Goodhue's lavish detail in the chancel of All Saints, Ashmont, for example, in 1897-99, is nothing less than the work of a decorative genius. And this was very fortunate for Cram, who remembered in his memoirs in 1936 that:

> what ability I had stopped short at one very definite point. I could see any architectural problem in its mass, proportion, composition and articulation, and visualize it in three dimensions, even before I set pencil to paper. I had also the faculty of planning, and I generally blocked out all our designs at quarter scale. There my ability ceased. I had neither the power nor the patience to work out any sort of decorative detail.[104]

Cram, however, who worked only with mass, scale, volume and void—the building, as it were, of space—thus found the alter ego he needed. And Goodhue's effervescent genius influenced him enormously. Or so at least Cram asserted many years after Goodhue's death when he wrote that his first tendencies, he knew, were "rather archaeological" and that "it was Goodhue who gave whatever came out of our office a quality of vitality. . . ."[105] Indeed, Cram was generous to a fault in his assessment of their relative contributions to their early work. He reported in his autobiography:

> Little by little we began to learn something from each other: he came to see problems more in the large, as consistent and unified conceptions, where detail was *only* a detail; while I slowly sloughed off some of my archaeological predispositions and realized the inherent value in his originality and modernism. While this process of cooperation and coordination helped vastly in the work we did at the time, it was in the end, curiously enough, the cause of our separation, for each of us came to look on himself as an individual designer with a definite desire to work things out, each in his own way. Very shortly we adopted the plan of dividing the work between us, he taking one project subject to my advice and consent in plan and composition, I another, up to the point where he applied all the decorative detail, where also I advised and approved.[106]

Cram's view of the matter, scarcely incredible or overweening, has nonetheless been widely discounted, though never openly disputed. *But it is now clear that it was Goodhue's view as well*, and that the same division of responsibility Cram refers to in his memoirs as between the two was still in effect after the opening of the New York Office. This is very evident in the Library's correspondence. A letter of Cram's to Goodhue on 25 August 1909 notes: ". . . when I can block out a rough plan, I will send it on to you so that you can begin to study it so far as its aesthetic expression is concerned."[107] Cram's usual "follow-up" criticism (in a different matter) is referred to by Goodhue in a letter to Ferguson of 15 March 1909: "R.A.C.'s suggested changes in the plan . . . were a great comfort and have been incorporated."[108] That Cram's part in all this was important to Goodhue is also evident in another letter to Ferguson of 25 January 1907: "I don't blame R.A.C. for his fierce letter of this morning," Goodhue wrote, "but though I could have notified him by 'phone as soon as I had read it, to stop work if he chose, I didn't do so, thinking that since he had gotten his mind fixed on the problem he had better keep it up and see what he could do."[109] Nor, however, need we take Cram's word alone now for the much debated terms of Cram and Goodhue's agreement as between the two offices with respect to West Point and St. Thomas: for we have now in Goodhue's own hand the exact agreement Cram reported in his memoirs. There is Goodhue's statement, written to both the other partners in his letter of 11 February 1910, in which he remarked that having "repeatedly expressed a good deal of satisfaction with the arrangement arrived at between the two offices," he would "for the sake of clarity formulate this as I understand it. . . ." He then dealt with the matter in question, explicitly noting that while the "working drawings specifications and general directions were to emanate from the New York Office," in the instances of both West Point and St. Thomas Church "all partners had an equal say." Moreover, in a letter to Cram of 15 April 1907, Goodhue confirmed the exact division of labor Cram later reported in his memoirs. Significantly, Goodhue was complaining, but about Cram having invaded *his* province, when he wrote: "I have understood hitherto that our work was so far as was possible divided into three departments—planning, construction and detail. *As to the two first,*" continued Goodhue, "*I have never questioned the ultimate authority of you both*"—this from the New York Office in the spring of 1907.

Actually, there was always a considerable rivalry in design between Cram and Goodhue, and never more so than in the case of St. Thomas. In fact, Cram always contended that he and Goodhue disagreed so profoundly about St. Thomas that each submitted totally different schemes for the whole church, and that the building committee accepted Cram's. That Cram and Goodhue often quietly submitted their own separate schemes while yet partners was discreetly but widely enough suspected at the time for Montgomery Schuyler to have referred to the practice in his "The Works of Cram, Goodhue and Ferguson" in *Architectural Record* in 1911. And that St. Thomas was a case of Cram's scheme having won it was well known enough for H. L. Bottomley to have flatly said so in *Architectural Record* in 1914. Thus George de Mille in his 1958 history of St. Thomas probably thought he was settling the issue when he quoted directly from the vestry minutes of the time that the plans for St. Thomas were thoroughly revised no less than *twelve times* because "Cram and Goodhue were in sharp disagreement as to many of the basic features of the plan. Cram won." But though de Mille naturally concluded that "the plan proper—size, proportions, mass—were the product of Cram's brain," he was naive to assume that a myth which so many have invested so much in for so long (else they might have to rethink so much) could be exploded merely by documentary evidence! This evidence has troubled no one, and one sees again and again in the business of Cram and Goodhue at St. Thomas the same sort of revisionism in the case of Cram's architectural practice that I tried to illustrate previously here in the case of Cram's architectural theory. Not very much more than a year ago, the architecture critic of *The New York Times*, for example, allowed himself this criticism of Walter Kidney's *The Architecture of Choice*:

> ... Kidney is also somewhat casual in his judgments of individual architects. There are rarely any strongly critical remarks, and he does not make the distinctions which, to me, seem necessary between the eclectics. He correctly says that Bertram Goodhue, architect of New York's St. Thomas Church, was a better architect than his onetime partner Ralph Cram, for example, and he notes that Goodhue worked well in many styles, but he never seems to grasp the fact that Goodhue was a tremendously creative design talent, while Cram was just a warmed-over gothic revivalist.[110]

60–61. *The First Stage of the Design Process* was Cram's, and his design initiatives invariably evolved from a series of quick, rough pencil sketches (usually in perspective though sometimes in elevation) that organized his thoughts and incited this very cerebral architect's imagination. Those reproduced above are a few of forty or so similar sketches by Cram in 1911 that deal with the nave and crossing of St. John The Divine.

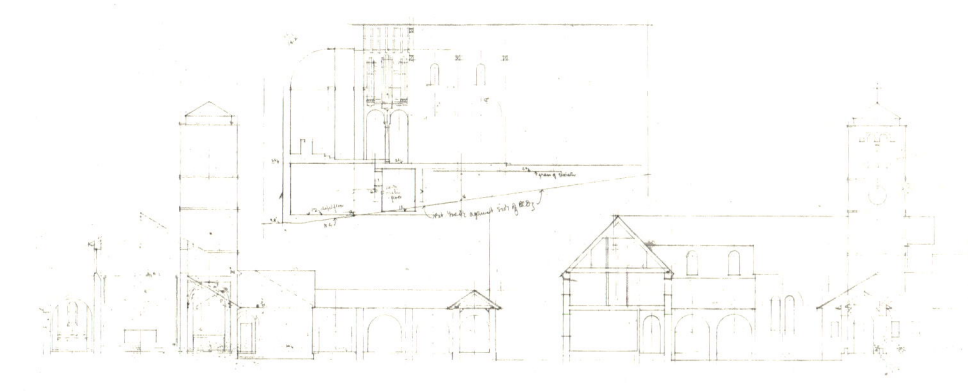

62. *The Second Stage of the Design Process* was also Cram's, and the most important. For Cram's "blocking out" of the building, always in plan and elevation, though thumbnail perspectives (as well as much mathematics) occur often in the margins, laid down the exact disposition of scale, mass, proportion, volume and void and the precise plan and organization of interior space from which his partners would develop the building. (Above, Cram's "brown strip" for the Chapel at Holy Cross Monastery, West Park, New York.)

63–64. *The Third Stage of the Design Process.* Here the initiative passed to Cram's partners, whose proposals for developing his masses and proportions were evolved through perspectives which Cram and his partners studied and criticized. The stylistic idiom to be used was usually studied first. In this case the Gothic scheme (left) of the Madison Avenue Church in New York did not recommend itself, and Cram chose instead the Byzantine scheme (right) finally built, to some extent because he wanted a "richness of color" that would survive New York's air pollution better than had the once silvery white stone of St. Thomas'.

65–66–67. *The Fourth Stage of the Design Process*, to some extent simultaneous with the third stage, was largely a matter of deciding in what terms style was to be couched. Here are three schemes for the tower of the East Liberty Church in Pittsburgh, each Gothic, but each quite different. Most fortunately Cram and his partners eschewed both the more archaeological and the more modernist variants for the splendid and vital design (below, right) that was finally realized.

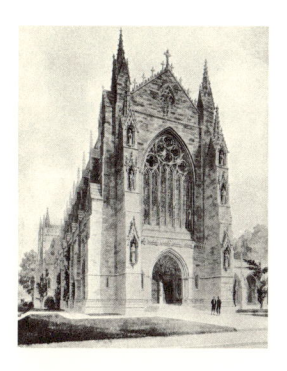

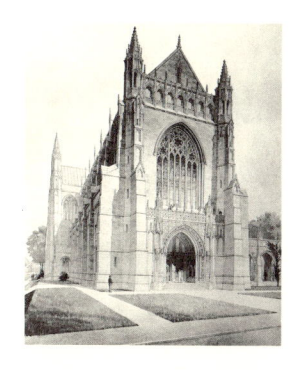

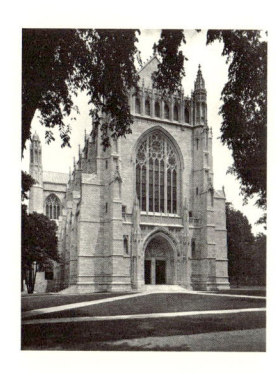

68–69–70. *The Fifth Stage of the Design Process* was the most subtle: how to select from a vast vocabulary the exactly right articulation of the agreed upon terms, the architectural *mot juste* Hoyle strove for in the Princeton Chapel perspectives above. Because Cram was out of the country at a crucial point we have his own reactions to Hoyle's final submission (center) in a letter that records a stage in the design process usually verbal and consequently normally undocumented. Cram asked Hoyle to crocket the gable, give the gable finial much more strength, add two more openings for a more vertical effect in the upper arcade (which Cram judged out of scale with the door and the window) and to lengthen the squat niches at the top of the lower part of the major western buttresses so that the weathering next below was omitted. The effect of these few but significant criticisms is easily seen in the chapel as built (right). This stage of the design process usually involved the making of a plaster model of the building, by means of which Cram and his partners tested their conclusions just prior to the beginning of working drawings.

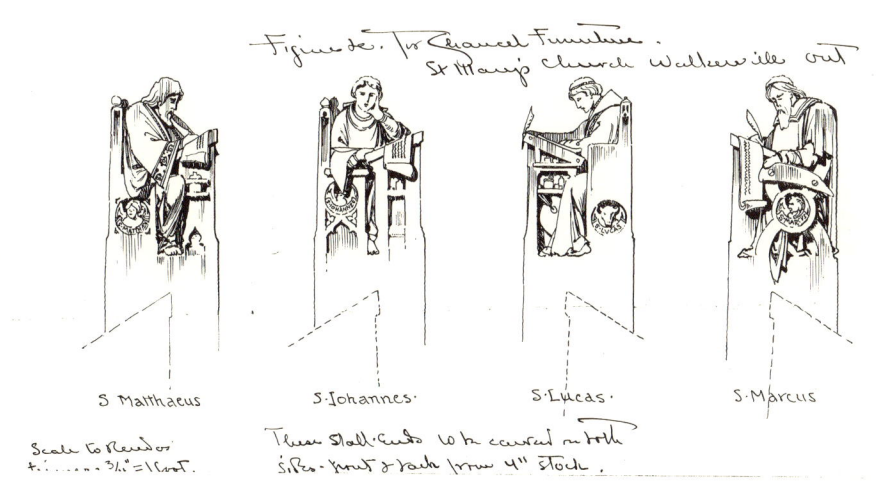

71. *Simultaneous Decorative Development.* During this five-stage design process another and similar sequence with respect to the interior was also developed. Every furnishing from candlesticks to hardware was carefully studied by the office, before Cram, who dealt closely with his artist-collaborators, invited them to submit the sketches (in the case of glass) or models (in the case of sculpture) they had worked up from the firm's schemes. These were never Cram's, but his partners', for Cram admitted he had neither the "power or patience" for detail. But Cram's rule—the graver and simpler and more restrained his masses the more detail he would allow his partners to propose—yielded splendid results: never more so than when Goodhue's decorative genius was a factor. (Above, right, Goodhue's studies for Kirchmayer of the figure sculpture in the chancel of St. Mary's, Walkerville, Ontario.)

59. The nave, St. John The Divine in New York

Perhaps we have all been more than "somewhat casual" as well in separating "fact" from opinion, which last need not be less interesting if it is well informed. Now, however, we have more evidence to study, which *may* settle the question. For in his letter to Cram of 15 April 1907, Goodhue refers definitely to the two schemes when he assures Cram that "if the Building Committee of St. Thomas' parish, when the two schemes are presented to them, reject my arrangement and choose yours, not one word of protest will come from me, and I rely upon you ... to take the same attitude." The unusual intensity with which they disagreed is also evident in Goodhue's rejoinders to Cram's previous letter: Goodhue insisted that "what you are pleased to term my lateral burrows are in reality pointed arches," and remarked that "it is unkind of you to call my theories outworn fads...." A crucial phrase reads: "little as I liked the interpolated gallery"—which refers of course, to the matter Cram dealt with in his memoirs where he remarked on the "deep gallery above, an innovation I had the daring to develop, and of which I have always been inordinately proud." By way of conclusion it may be useful to add that Goodhue's remark in a letter to Cram of 30 April 1907, that "I shouldn't care to see my plan with R.A.C.'s cross section, and his cross section for my plan is manifestly an impossibility," indicates the wide divergence of the two schemes, and that in a letter to Cram of two years later, on 11 February 1910, Goodhue is clearly under the impression that Cram's design won out. He wrote on that date to Cram that "... in the case of St. Thomas, I was and still am thoroughly dissatisfied.... I believe that I produced a better plan than the accepted one, at the same time succeeding in eliminating the side gallery which ... I cannot consider other than an extremely objectionable feature."

Goodhue, moreover, according to Frank Cleveland, a junior partner, took the decision badly. In a letter to Cram Cleveland remembered that shortly thereafter "BGG went to Montecito to rest up or drown his sorrows, I never knew which...." Yet, wrote Cleveland, Goodhue returned to the office "with surprising new vigor and the whole office snap[ped] out of the stalemate and [went] about creating the church that has become famous as a ... real work of creative architecture." Still, the bitterness engendered was no small reason for Cram and Goodhue's breakup. And this, wrote Cleveland to Cram in the same letter, in 1936, was rather a tragedy because "the feud was only the jealousies between office forces and should not have sunk in so deeply on part of the members of the firm. Both offices," Cleveland thought, "were 'kidding' each of their respective 'bosses', who were taking it seriously." Nonetheless, allowed Cleveland, who knew both Cram and Goodhue did their best work when forced by each other to argue for their predilections, "as a result the church is glorious. I am not sure a better has been built since."[111]

I do not, of course, contend that Ralph Adams Cram personally developed every idea and drew every detail of every building during his long life that bears his name. Van Rensselaer's description of Richardson's practice could not be improved upon in Cram's case: Cram's role was threefold—"initiative impulse, constant criticism and final oversight."[112] Interestingly enough, the pressures of a large practice forced Goodhue in New York to exactly the same system: like Cram, he sketched, blocked out, suggested and then criticized the development of his ideas by trusted draughtsmen. "I don't try at all any more to draw at the office,"[113] Goodhue wrote to Cram in 1907, and emphasized this point two years later, in a letter to Cram of 22 July 1909 when he complained that Cram was expecting too much of him because ". . . three of the best men here and there to whom I could look for actual designing from my suggestions are as you know in England for the summer. . . . This leaves me with only second class men (on the designing side, that is) to do the work." But it would be absurd to suggest that Cram should have—or needed—to do more. Every important church or collegiate design of the Cram office began on Cram's sketch pad,[114] and never reached his partners until he had developed his sketches into the famous "brown strips," many of which survive, on which he would block out in elevation and plan (checking himself constantly with numerous thumbnail perspectives in the margins) the building in question.[115] Volume and void, mass and proportion, fenestration and the areas where detail might occur, with sometimes its general character indicated as well, all this was done before his partners ever got a whack at the detailed development Cram depended on them for, though in the give and take of a constant mutual criticism thereafter one naturally loses sight of specific roles. Even after the work had gone to the drafting room Cram might intervene: John Nicholas Brown remembers Cram completely redrawing the tower of St. George's School in a few moments, and the difference, Brown remembered, was "astounding."[116] Another example is also at hand, thanks to the fact that Cram was in Europe at a crucial stage in the final development of Princeton Chapel and had to write back his criticisms (in a letter now in the Library's collection) of the perspective Hoyle mailed him.[117] I reproduce that perspective here together with a photograph of the chapel as built. Notice the change in the niches of the buttresses of the west front; the introduction of a bolder finial on the gable and of crockets; and the more vertical aspect of the upper arcade. These were Cram's three criticisms, and they made rather a difference.

There was still another role Cram played. Though he had neither skill or patience in conceiving detail, he knew exactly what he wanted, and how to get it from his artist-collaborators—with whom he worked closely on the detailed plans his partners had worked out.[118] He was a perceptive and learned critic, demanding but also enthusiastic, for Cram's concept of a building as an organic unity of all the arts required a constant attention to all the detail. But his power over his craftsmen—some of whom, like Charles Connick, he had helped to get started and to evolve into major figures in their own right—was legendary.

John Angel, whose work Cram admired to excess, commented on this in a letter to Cleveland after Cram's death. Cleveland's reply has survived and provides an important insight into the subtle nature of Cram's role in the office. The italics are my own.

> Your letter on the occasion of Mr. Cram's death was a very just estimate of the qualities which made him so remarkable. A gentleman of great experience, connected with one of the institutions for which we have worked, said that he had never met anyone who could so powerfully communicate his enthusiasm to a group; it was, he said, a sort of electric radiation which really inspired the men to whom he was speaking. This was, of course, a group of laymen; in the case of artists and craftsmen, the effect was doubly remarkable because *Mr. Cram made them believe in themselves and in their ability to carry out his plans.*[119]

Here one sees another and more subtle way in which Cram made his influence felt. "Initiative impulse, constant criticism, final oversight": we now know that Cram was the dominant influence in all but the strictly "New York Office" work of the firm. Moreover, this controversy having been now put behind us, both Cram and Goodhue—who remained fast friends, incidentally, after what Goodhue called their "divorce," and on several occasions seriously considered working together again at West Point—may now in the wake of this new documentation emerge, finally, for what they really were. Nor is *either* likely to disappoint.

I have asserted here, by way of explanation for our somewhat tardy rediscovery of Ralph Adams Cram, that the scarcely credible and certainly remarkable range of Cram's several vocations, together with Goodhue's more obviously architectural ability, had the effect of undermining Cram's reputation as a designer in his own lifetime and contributed as well to the sense of his posterity that Cram's life was more legendary than factual; and that after his death both these and other factors facilitated the understandable but now increasingly suspect revisionism the modernists would have us accept as history. Furthermore, I have argued that by shaping Cram in our minds' eyes today much the same way his contemporaries did, we may repeat all over again, despite the fact that we now have evidence to the contrary his peers did not, the same mistakes the modernists capitalized upon; all the more so as we will only with difficulty free ourselves from the modernist view of Cram because he was no more a Victorian than a modernist, and may not for awhile, therefore, intrigue a body of interested opinion significant enough to effect his rehabilitation as an architect, however much we may concede to him in other respects. Fundamentally, however, I have sought here to document the underlying assumption of both the exhibition and this essay: that his view of Cram's life is an impoverishing one for us as for Cram, and that this generation must now seek for Cram, who was unarguably the great American architect of the century in his field, both a fairer hearing and a more precise criticism. But there yet remains the question of his power of design. Clearly, that is a subject for a larger work than this. Yet some indication of the treasure that may be disclosed by further inquiry is again available to us in the measure a small band of discerning professional contemporaries took of Cram's best work, after his and Goodhue's breakup, at St. John The Divine in New York.

When first Cram wrote to Goodhue of their probable opportunity at St. John's, Goodhue's rejoinder was enthusiastic but perceptive: he wondered "what in the world we could do if we were forced to adhere to the present foundations."[120] Cram—after the dissolution of their partnership—faced exactly that problem, and yet persuaded those foundations to a remarkable service. By his introduction of smaller intermediate piers in the primary arcade Cram resolved the nave into a system of four great squares or double bays, rather than eight rectangular bays; and by lifting these and the primary piers to relatively an enormous height (the intermediate piers are five feet in diameter to a height of nearly one hundred feet) and by then pushing back the clerestory to a secondary line of piers and lifting the aisles in between to the full height of the nave vault, he not only achieved an unprecedented amplitude (double that of any medieval cathedral) as well as a dramatic height and a remarkable play of light and shade, but was able to provide most of the necessary support for the vault within the building and thus to eliminate the flying arches he doubted could for long withstand the New York climate, and for the first time to express the alternating thrusts and stresses of a sexpartite vault on the exterior by the doubling of his buttresses where the diagonal and transverse ribs concentrate.[121] In these last respects particularly, A. D. F. Hamlin of Columbia, often a severe critic of Cram's ideas, was enormously impressed—writing publicly that he could not "do justice to the technical brilliancy and originality of this design, by which the greater part of the abutment of the colossal 56-foot vault is provided within the edifice. . . ." He concluded: "Nothing comparable to this superb design has ever been executed or conceived in America, and the cathedrals of Europe may fairly be challenged to surpass or even to equal it. . . . The French Gothic as here used is handled with such originality and boldness of invention as to form in reality a new and distinctly American chapter in its development."[122] At the same time, A. Kingsley Porter of Harvard wrote to Ralph Adams Cram:

> Your nave is glorious—in its half built state I can see that it will realize much more than all the beauty I at once felt in the drawings. Your design surpasses what the Gothic builders achieved in their to me superlative effect—the vista through openings at openings beyond. If you can get the same inspired execution for the nave that you did for the baptistry, you will have written a tenth symphony.[123]

The background of Porter's assertion is also important, and I have Walter Muir

Whitehill's permission to quote here from a letter of his of 31 July 1974 that is very pertinent. He wrote of Porter's letter to Cram:

> It seems to me a document of the highest importance for a number of reasons. By 1926 Porter had been working for a dozen years on Romanesque architecture and sculpture. His Gothic studies were all well behind him. He was a man of highly critical tastes not given to easy and exaggerated praise. He disliked Roman architecture and everything that was produced in France in the 19th century. When he spoke well of anything it was from conviction after careful thought. He shared none of Cram's religious interest and was therefore not concerned with the New York cathedral as a place for the use of the Episcopal Church. He was simply looking at it as a piece of architecture and as such he praised it in the highest terms.[124]

It is perhaps scarcely fair of me to have cited in conclusion only Cram's masterpiece. But the reader will understand that I have judged a strong incentive necessary if we are to overcome the mythology of Cram and deal with him in his to me chief dignity—as an architect. And this New York nave, unarguably Cram's alone in concept, and the more remarkable for the fact that it was achieved despite foundations that startled even Goodhue's imagination, surely cannot fail to incite us to this task. For one sees in its grandeur of space and color what Kingsley Porter meant: one recognizes an ideal, always fervent, that is suddenly lucid.

NOTES

RAC = Ralph Adams Cram
AA/BPL = Architectural Archive, Boston Public Library

1. Clippings of these obituaries were found among R.A.C.'s papers in 1975 and are in the AA/BPL. All newspaper obituaries ran in the early editions of 23 Sept. 1942 except those from the *Washington Star* and *New York World Telegram* (late editions, 22 Sept.). *The New York Times* editorial ran on 24 Sept.; *The Times* (of London) on 24 Sept. 1942.

2. Alex. Hoyle to W. Watkin, undated letter ca. Nov. 1942. AA/BPL.

3. Wayne Andrews. "American Gothic" in *American Heritage*, vol. XXII, no. 6, Oct. 1971, p. 97.

4. Joseph Hudnut to R.A.C., letter of 10 Dec. 1938. AA/BPL.

5. A partial checklist of R.A.C.'s buildings and published works follows these notes.

6. Douglass Shand Tucci, *All Saints', Ashmont, Dorchester, Boston: A Centennial History* (Boston, 1975), p. 80, notes 49, 50.

7. Dean of Sisters College at Catholic University of America to R.A.C., letter of 28 April 1919. AA/BPL.

8. Bishop James H. Ryan is quoted in an undated sales brochure of Marshall Jones Co., for R.A.C.'s *Convictions and Controversies*. AA/BPL.

9. Hilaire Belloc. Introduction to R.A.C.'s *The Catholic Church and Art* (New York: MacMillan, 1930), p. 7.

10. The *San Francisco Monitor* is quoted in an undated sales brochure of Marshall Jones Co., for R.A.C.'s *Convictions and Controversies*. AA/BPL.

11. A series of papers were published by Marshall Jones Co. in 1920 under the title *A Tribute to Dr. Ralph Adams Cram from Holy Cross College*. A copy survives in the Guiney Collection at Holy Cross Library. (Guiney was an early and important influence on Cram and a lifelong friend.)

12. An undated loose newspaper clipping announcing the election of Cram, Millay and Sandburg exists in the AA/BPL.

13. The twelfth edition consisted of the eleventh edition and three new volumes published in 1922.

14. President of M.I.T. to R.A.C., letter of 20 June 1914. AA/BPL.

15. Bernard Berenson to R.A.C., letter of 2 June 1941. AA/BPL.

16. George Coffman to John Nicholas Brown, letter of 6 Oct. 1942. AA/BPL.

17. E. K. Rand to R.A.C., letter of 2 Dec. 1938. AA/BPL.

18. Brooks Adams to R.A.C., letter of 11 Nov. 1914. AA/BPL.

19. Herman T. Radin. *The Medical Pickwick*, Oct. 1918, p. 400.

20. Albert Jay Nock to R.A.C., letter of 4 April ca. 1940. AA/BPL.

21. P. W. Voltz to R.A.C., letter of 18 Dec. 1934. AA/BPL.

22. R.A.C. to the Editor of *The Transcript*, 26 Oct. 1914.

23. No connection between the Calvert Series and the Calvert Associates has been documented.

24. Loose clipping, dated only 21 May in Cram scrapbook, from the Boston *Herald*. See also *New York World Telegram* obituary of Cram, 22 Sept. 1942.

25. Dean of Sisters College at Catholic University of America to R.A.C., letter of 28 April 1919.

26. T. R. Shields to R.A.C., letter of 2 May 1934.

27. Ms of letter of R.A.C. to the Editor of *The Transcript*, dated only 19 Oct.

28. Several of his most important addresses will be found in R.A.C.'s *The Ministry of Art*.

29. *The Times* (of London) *Literary Supplement*, 30 March 1916, p. 141.

30. Ralph Adams Cram. *The Heart of Europe* (New York: Scribner's, 1915), pp. 3, 98–99.

31. Marian Nichols to R.A.C., letter of 29 April, ca. 1895; letter of Mrs. Fred Bullard to R.A.C., undated. Both AA/BPL.

32. The Cram Collection is rich in memorabilia of this period.
33. H. T. Parker to R.A.C., letter of 29 June 1916. AA/BPL.
34. George H. Allen. "Yankee Medievalist" in *Architectural Forum*, vol. 55, July 1931, pp. 79–80.
35. See *Harvard Magazine*, vol. 78, no. 1, Sept. 1975, p. 11. See also Douglass Shand Tucci. *Church Building in Boston* (Concord, N.H.: Rumford Press for the Trustees of The Dorchester Savings Bank, 1975), pp. 85–114, *passim*.
36. Douglass Shand Tucci. "Ralph Adams Cram and the Boston Gothicists: A Reappraisal," a paper given to the Annual Meeting of the Society of Architectural Historians, April 1975, an abstract of which will be found in the October issue of the *Journal of the Society of Architectural Historians*; Robert Muccigrosso. "American Gothic: Ralph Adams Cram" in *Thought*, the Fordham University Quarterly, vol. XLVII, no. 184, March 1972, pp. 102–118; Peter Williams. "Two Golden Ages: Elitism and Medieval Nostalgia in the New England Imagination," unpub. paper at Library of Miami University, Oxford, Ohio.
37. Walter Taylor. "Protestant Churches" in *Forms and Functions of 20th Century Architecture* (Talbot Hamlin, ed.) (New York, 1952), vol. III, chap. 10, pp. 335–336.
38. Lewis Mumford. *Sticks and Stones* (New York: Dover edition, 1955), p. 91.
39. Gerald Allen. "The Fourth St. Thomas Church" in *Architectural Record*, April 1974, p. 113.
40. Jay Sadler. *The Gothic Revival: The Only Proper Style*. Typescript of forthcoming book to be published by New York Graphic Society.
41. Ms of address by R.A.C. at St. Paul's Cathedral, Boston, 15 Oct. 1933. AA/BPL.
42. Ralph Adams Cram. *The Ministry of Art* (Boston: Houghton Mifflin, 1914), p. 37.
43. Ibid., p. 119.
44. Ralph Adams Cram. *My Life in Architecture* (Boston: Little, Brown, 1936), p. 32.
45. For a discussion of Vaughan's role as R.A.C.'s local mentor see *Church Building in Boston*, part 2, chap. 5, pp. 85–94. See also William Morgan. *The Architecture of Henry Vaughan* (Ann Arbor, Mich.: University Microfilms, 1972).
46. R.A.C.'s unpublished journal of 1885 (unpaged). AA/BPL.
47. Ralph Adams Cram. *Church Building* (Boston: Small, Maynard and Co., 1899), p. 247.
48. Ibid., p. 13.
49. *The Ministry of Art*, p. 123
50. Montgomery Schuyler. *The Works of Cram, Goodhue and Ferguson* (New York, entire issue of *Architectural Record* for Jan 1911, vol. XXIX, no. 1), p. 87. Cf. Alfred Tapan North. *Ralph Adams Cram* (New York: McGraw Hill, 1931), p. 3.
51. This paragraph appeared in somewhat different form in *Church Building in Boston*.
52. Ralph Adams Cram. Editorial in *Christian Art*, April 1907, p. 20.
53. N. F. Cachemaille-Day. "Church and Community" in *Post-War Church Building* (E. M. Short, ed.) (London: Hollis and Carter, 1947), p. 39.
54. Ralph Adams Cram. "All Saints' Church, Ashmont" in *The Churchman*, vol. XXIX, 15 Apr. 1899, p. 589.
55. Phoebe Stanton. *Pugin* (New York: Viking Press, 1972), p. 85.
56. Ralph Adams Cram. "Architecture" in *The New Parish Church of All Saints* (Boston, 1892), p. 12.
57. Ibid.
58. "All Saints' Church, Ashmont," in *The Churchman*, p. 561.
59. Ibid.
60. For a more complete discussion, see *Church Building in Boston*, pp. 58–59.
61. Wallace Sabine. *Collected Papers on Acoustics* (Cambridge: Harvard University Press; London: Humphrey Milford, Oxford University Press, 1922), pp. 208–209.
62. *The Ministry of Art*, p. 59.
63. Untitled MS by R.A.C., dated 4 May 1938.
64. *The Ministry of Art*, p. 62.
65. Ralph Adams Cram. Introduction to P. H. Ditchfield's *Picturesque English Cottages and Their Dooryard Gardens* (Philadelphia: John C. Winston Co., 1905).
66. Ralph Adams Cram. *The Catholic Church and Art* (New York: MacMillan, 1930), p. 106.
67. *The Catholic Church and Art*, pp. 105–106.
68. *My Life in Architecture*, p. 274.
69. *The Catholic Church and Art*, p. 106.
70. *My Life in Architecture*, p. 267.

71. From a loose, undated clipping in R.A.C.'s scrapbook of an interview given in St. Louis in 1934. AA/BPL. Cf. *My Life in Architecture*, p. 270.
72. *My Life in Architecture*, p. 268.
73. See note 71 above; cf. *My Life in Architecture*, p. 270.
74. *My Life in Architecture*, p. 282.
75. See note 71 above.
76. Ralph Adams Cram. "American Architecture" in the *Encyclopaedia Britannica* (12th ed., 1922), vol. 30, p. 187.
77. *My Life in Architecture*, p. 257.
78. From a loose, undated clipping in R.A.C.'s scrapbook of an interview he gave to the *Roswell Daily Record* in Arizona. Cf. *The Ministry of Art*, p. 36.
79. *The Catholic Church and Art*, p. 23.
80. See note 71 above.
81. *The Ministry of Art*, p. 121.
82. *My Life in Architecture*, p. 268.
83. *The Ministry of Art*, p. 121.
84. Ibid., p. 120.
85. *My Life in Architecture*, p. 169.
86. *The Catholic Church and Art*, p. 107.
87. *My Life in Architecture*, p. 274.
88. Ibid., p. 275.
89. *The Catholic Church and Art*, pp. 107–108.
90. Ibid., p. 112.
91. *My Life in Architecture*, p. 279.
92. Untitled and undated MS in AA/PBL.
93. *Church Building*, p. 84.
94. Ibid., p. 85.
95. Untitled MS dated 4 May 1938 in AA/PBL.
96. *The Ministry of Art*, pp. 35–36.
97. Edward J. Sutfin and Maurice Lavanoux. "Contemporary Catholic Architecture" in *Modern Church Architecture* (Albert Christ-Janer and Mary Mix Foley, eds.) (New York: McGraw Hill, 1962), p. 1.
98. Harold E. Wagoner. "A New Religiosity? Sensate Chaos? or What the Heck is Happening To Church Building" in *Faith and Form*, vol. VIII, Spring 1975, p. 8.
99. Margaret Henderson Floyd. Review of *Church Building in Boston* to appear in a forthcoming issue of *The Journal of the Society of Architectural Historians*.

100. *Sticks and Stones*, p. 91.
101. *Century Memorials, 1942* (New York, 1943), p. 21.
102. "Belligerent Gothicist" in *Fortune*, vol. II, no. 6, Dec. 1931, p. 77.
103. Ralph Adams Cram. *The End of Democracy* (Boston: Marshall Jones Co., 1937), p. 74.
104. *My Life in Architecture*, pp. 77–78.
105. Ibid., p. 78.
106. Ibid., pp. 78–79.
107. Cf. *My Life in Architecture*, p. 78.
108. This is, of course, a case of a job where Goodhue was in charge.
109. There is unfortunately no indication of what work B.G.G. is referring to.
110. Paul Goldberger. Review of Walter Kidney's *The Architecture of Choice* in *The New York Times Book Review*, 28 July 1974, p. 4.
111. Frank Cleveland to R.A.C., undated letter in AA/BPL. As Cleveland answers questions posed by R.A.C. at the time he was writing his memoirs, the letter is ca. 1935.
112. Mariana van Rensselaer. *Henry Hobson Richardson and His Works* (New York: Dover edition, 1969, with an Introduction by William Morgan), p. 123.
113. Bertram Goodhue to R.A.C., letter of 26 Nov. 1907. AA/BPL.
114. *Church Building in Boston*, p. 67. A letter to the author of 17 April 1975 by John T. Doran that covers this matter is in the AA/BPL.
115. Some of these are illustrated on page 31 here.
116. Mr. John Nicholas Brown to the author, letter of 19 Nov. 1973. AA/BPL.
117. This perspective is reproduced here on page 33.
118. *Church Building in Boston*, pp. 70–71.
119. Frank Cleveland to John Angel, letter of 28 Sept. 1942. AA/BPL.
120. Bertram Goodhue to R.A.C., letter of 24 Oct. 1907. AA/BPL.
121. This paragraph appeared in somewhat more rudimentary form in *Church Building in Boston*.
122. A. D. F. Hamlin. *A Study of the Designs for The Cathedral of St. John The Divine* (New York, 1924).
123. A. Kingsley Porter to R.A.C., letter of 22 June 1926. AA/BPL.
124. Walter Muir Whitehill to the author, letter of 31 July 1974. AA/BPL.

CHECKLISTS AND BIBLIOGRAPHY

A complete checklist of Cram's buildings and published works can scarcely be compiled for many years. The checklists that follow, however, include all of his important work and are thought to be accurate save only in the case of omissions, with these exceptions. Cram's work was so extensive and each individual building was carried on for so long a period of time that any attempt at dating his buildings at this point would confuse rather than clarify, and after experimentation with several systems, I have thought it best to simply omit any dates at all until a really accurate list can be compiled. There are virtues to an incomplete checklist; there are none at all to vague dates. Secondly, no attempt at all has been made to list any of the firm's decorative work (altar crosses, reredoses and such) or to list any of the hundreds of published plates and articles on the firm's work. Though I would have preferred to omit New York Office and Boston Office attributions because these (like the dates I might have incorporated) rest on no real authority at all, the subject seemed too sensitive, however, and where there is some ground or other to do so I have noted 1902–14 work as Boston (*) or New York (**). These are not reliable attributions, however, in the strict sense.

1. CHURCHES WHOLLY DESIGNED BY THE FIRM

Episcopal Churches

  **All Saints' Cathedral, Halifax, N.S., Canada
  All Saints' Church, Brookline, Mass.
  All Saints' Church, Dorchester, Boston
  All Saints' Church, Peterborough, N.H.
  Calvary Church, Americus, Ga.
 *Calvary Church, Pittsburgh, Pa.
  Cathedral Church of St. John The Divine, New York City
    Nave
    West Front (incomplete)
    North Transept (incomplete)
    South Transept (not started)
    Crossing and Tower (not started)
    Baptistry
    St. Martin's Chapel
    Choir (additions)
    Synod House
    Bishop's House
    Deanery
 **Chapel of The Intercession, New York City
  Christ Church, Hyde Park, Boston
 **Christ Church, West Haven, Conn.
  Church of Our Saviour, Middleboro, Mass.
  Convent Church and Monastery, Cambridge, Mass.
  Emmanuel Church, Champaign, Ill.
  Emmanuel Church, Newport, R.I.
 *Holy Cross Monastery and Chapel, West Park, N.Y.
  St. Anne's Chapel, Arlington Heights, Mass.
 *St. Elizabeth's Chapel, Sudbury, Mass.
  St. James Church, Lake Delaware, N.Y.
 **St. John's Church, West Hartford, Conn.
  St. Luke's Chapel (now SS. John and James), Roxbury, Boston
  St. Mark's Cathedral, Hastings, Nebraska
 **St. Mark's Church, Mt. Kisco, N.Y.
  St. Mary's Church, Walkerville, Ont., Canada
 *St. Paul's Cathedral, Detroit, Michigan
  St. Paul's Church, Brockton, Mass.
  St. Paul's Church, Malden, Mass.
  St. Paul's Church, Winston Salem, N.C.
  St. Paul's Church, Yonkers, N.Y.
  St. Stephen's Church, Cohasset, Mass.
  St. Stephen's Church, Fall River, Mass.
  St. Thomas Church, New York City
 **Trinity Church, Havana, Cuba

Roman Catholic Churches

  Church of SS. Peter and Paul, Fall River, Mass.
  Holy Rosary Church, Pittsburgh, Pa.
  Sacred Heart, Jersey City, N.J.
  St. Florian's Church, Detroit, Mich.
  St. Mary's, Detroit, Mich.

Protestant Churches

  Central Union Church, Honolulu, Hawaii
  Christ Church (Methodist), New York City
  Church of The Covenant, Cleveland, Ohio
  East Congregational Church, Grand Rapids, Mich.
  East Liberty Church, Pittsburgh, Pa.
 **First Baptist Church, Pittsburgh, Pa.
  First Evangelical Lutheran Church, Louisville, Ky.
  First Presbyterian Church, Greensburg, Pa.
  First Presbyterian Church, Jamestown, N.Y.
  First Presbyterian Church, Lincoln, Neb.
  First Presbyterian Church, Utica, N.Y.

First Presbyterian Church, Tacoma, Wash.
First Presbyterian Church, Glens Falls, N.Y.
First Unitarian Church, West Newton, Mass.
First Universalist Church, Somerville, Mass.
Fourth Presbyterian Church, Chicago, Ill.
Grace Lutheran Church, Fremont, Ohio
House of Good Hope Church, St. Paul, Minn.
Newton Center Methodist Church, Newton, Mass.
Phillips Congregational Church, Exeter, N.H.
Second Church, Unitarian, Boston (now Ruggles St. Church)
Swedenborgian Church, Bryn Athyn, Pa.
Swedenborgian Church, Newton, Mass.
Trinity Methodist Church, Durham, N.C.

School Chapels

Choate School Chapel, Wallingford, Conn.
St. George's School Chapel, Newport, R.I.
Mercersburg School Chapel, Mercersburg, Pa.
Princeton University Chapel, Princeton, N.J.
Rollins College Chapel, Winter Park, Fla.
United States Military Academy Chapel, West Point, N.Y.
University of the South Chapel, Sewanee, Tenn.
Wheaton College Chapel, Norton, Mass.

Mortuary Chapels

Cemetery Chapel, Norwood, Mass.
Englewood Chapel, Nahant, Mass.
War Memorial Chapel, Belleau Wood, France

2. IMPORTANT ADDITIONS BY FIRM TO CHURCHES BY OTHER ARCHITECTS

Episcopal Churches

*All Saints, Worcester, Mass.
Cathedral Church of St. Paul, Boston
Christ Church Cathedral, Hartford, Conn.
Church of The Advent, Boston
**Grace Church, Chicago, Ill.
Grace Church, Lawrence, Mass.
Grace Church, Manchester, N.H.
Grace Church, Providence, R.I.
*Holy Spirit Church, Dorchester, Boston
St. James Church, New York City
St. James Church, Roxbury, Boston (destroyed)
St. John's, Beverly Farms, Mass.
St. John The Evangelist, Boston
St. John's Church, Newport, R.I.
St. John's Church, Providence, R.I.
St. Luke's Cathedral, Portland, Me.
St. Michael's Church, Milton, Mass.
St. Paul's Church, Chicago, Ill.
St. Paul's Church, Pawtucket, R.I.
St. Stephen's Church, Westborough, Mass.
Trinity Church, Princeton, N.J.

Roman Catholic Churches

Gate of Heaven Church, South Boston, Mass.
St. Ignatius Church, New York City
St. Mary's Cathedral, Peoria, Ill.
St. Paul's Church, Brooklyn, New York City
St. Vincent de Paul, Los Angeles, Calif.

Protestant Churches

All Souls Unitarian, Lowell, Mass.
Independent Presbyterian Church, Savannah, Ga.
Leyden Congregational Church, Brookline, Mass.
Pine Street Presbyterian Church, Harrisburg, Pa.
**Sage Memorial Chapel, Far Rockaway, N.Y.

School Chapels

St. Paul's School Chapel, Concord, N.H.

3. CHURCHES BY OTHER ARCHITECTS FOR WHICH CRAM AND FERGUSON WERE CONSULTING ARCHITECTS.

Grace Cathedral, San Francisco, Calif.
National Cathedral, Washington, D.C.

4. COLLEGES AND SCHOOLS FOR WHICH CRAM DID MAJOR WORK
(Supervisory role)

*Boston University, Boston (School of Theology, etc.)
Notre Dame University, Indiana (dining hall, etc.)
Phillips Exeter Academy, Exeter, N.H. (dormitories, etc.)
*Princeton University, Princeton, N.J. (chapel, graduate college)
*Rice Institute, Houston, Texas (dormitories, etc.)
Rollins College, Winter Park, Fla. (chapel, etc.)
*Sweet Briar College, Sweet Briar, Va. (dormitories, etc.)
**Taft School, Watertown, Conn.
*United States Military Academy, West Point, N.Y. (chapel, etc.)
*University of Richmond, Richmond, Va. (dormitories, etc.)
University of Southern California, Los Angeles, Calif. (library)
University of the South, Sewanee, Tenn. (chapel)
*Wellesley College, Wellesley, Mass. (alumnae bldg.)
*Wheaton College, Norton, Mass. (chapel, library, etc.)
*Williams College, Williamstown, Mass. (library, etc.)

5. MISCELLANEOUS WORK OF SOME NOTE

    Attwood House and gallery, Gloucester, Mass.
    Barron House, Back Bay, Boston
    Beebe Memorial Library, Wakefield, Mass.
**Economy Concrete Co. Building, New Haven, Conn.
**"El Fureidis," Santa Barbara, Calif.
    Federal Building, Boston
**Goodhue House, New York City
 *Guild Steps, Boston
 *"Harborcourt," Brown Estate, Newport, R.I.
    Japanese garden court, Museum of Fine Arts, Boston
    Knapp House, New Bedford, Mass.
 *Mather School, Dorchester, Boston
    Misses Masters' School, Dobbs Ferry, N.Y.
    Nashua Public Library, Nashua, N.H.
    Parker Hill Branch, Boston Public Library, Boston
    Peoples Savings Bank, Providence, R.I.
    Provident Mutual Building, Philadelphia, Pa.
    Richmond Court Apartments, Brookline, Mass.
    Sayles Public Library, Pawtucket, R.I.
    Sewall House, Houston, Texas
**Washington Hotel, Colon, Panama
    Watkins House, Winong, Ill.
    "Whitehall" (additions), Cram House, Sudbury, Mass.

6. PARTIAL CHECKLIST OF CRAM'S PUBLISHED WORKS

Books

English Country Churches (Boston: Bates and Guild, 1898)
The Decadent (Boston: Copeland and Day, 1901; there was an 1893 edition, privately printed for the author)
Black Spirits and White (Chicago: Stone and Kimball, 1901)
Church Building (Boston: Small, Maynard and Co., 1901)
Church Building (Boston: Marshall Jones and Co., 1914 and 1924)
The Ruined Abbeys of Great Britain (New York: J. Potts, 1906)
The Ruined Abbeys of Great Britain (Boston: Marshall Jones Co., 1927)
Impressions of Japanese Architecture and the Allied Arts (Boston: Marshall Jones Co., 1906)
The Gothic Quest (Boston: Baker and Taylor Co., 1907)
American Country Houses of Today (New York: Architectural Book Publishing Co., 1913)
Excalibur (Boston: Richard C. Badger, The Gorham Press, 1909)
The Ministry of Art (Boston: Houghton Mifflin, 1914)
Heart of Europe (New York: Scribners, 1915)
The Substance of Gothic (Boston: Marshall Jones Co., 1917)
The Nemesis of Mediocrity (Boston: Marshall Jones Co., 1917)
Six Lectures on Architecture (co-author) (University of Chicago Press, 1917)
The Great Thousand Years (Boston: Marshall Jones Co., 1918)
The Sins of the Fathers (Boston: Marshall Jones Co., 1919)
Walled Towns (Boston: Marshall Jones Co., 1919, 1920)
Gold, Frankincense and Myrrh (Boston: Marshall Jones Co., 1919)
Towards the Great Peace (Boston: Marshall Jones Co., 1922)
The Significance of the Fine Arts (co-author) (Boston: Marshall Jones Co., for A.I.A., 1923). Cram's chapter: pp. 59–115
American Church Architecture of Today (editor) (New York: Architectural Book Publishing Co., 1929)
The Catholic Church and Art (New York: MacMillan, 1930)
The Cathedral of Palma de Mallorca (Medieval Academy of America, 1933)
Convictions and Controversies (Boston: Marshall Jones Co., 1935)
My Life in Architecture (Boston: Little Brown & Co., 1936)
The End of Democracy (Boston: Marshall Jones Co., 1937)

Books Known to Have Been Prefaced by Cram

Henry Adams. *Mont-Saint Michel and Chartres* (Boston: Houghton Mifflin, 1914)
F. Bligh Bond. *The Hill of Vision* (Boston: Marshall Jones Co., 1919)
L. B. Bridahan. *Gargoyles, Chimeres and the Grotesque in French Gothic Sculpture* (New York: Architectural Book Publishing Co., 1930)
P. H. Ditchfield. *Picturesque English Cottages and Their Dooryard Gardens* (Philadelphia: John C. Winston Co., 1905)
Leon V. Solon. *Polychromy* (New York: Architectural Book Publishing Co., 1924)
L. P. Soule. *Spanish Farm Houses and Minor Public Buildings* (New York, 1924)
F. R. Weber. *Church Symbolism* (Cleveland: J. H. Jansen, 1927)

Anthologies or Reference Works to Which Cram Was a Contributor

Affirmations (Bernard Bell, ed.) (New York: Sheed, 1938)
Bertram Grosvenor Goodhue: Master of Many Arts (New York: A.I.A. Press, 1925)
Careers in the Making (I. M. Robertson, ed.) (New York: Harper, 1942)
Dictionary of Architecture and Building (Russell Sturgis, ed.) (New York: MacMillan, 1902)
Encyclopedia Britannica (12th ed.), 1922, vol. xxx
Essays and Addresses Toward a Liberal Education (A. C. Baird, ed.) (Boston: Ginn, 1934)
Essays Toward Truth (Kenneth Allen, ed.) (New York: Holt, 1924)
Farm Houses, Manor Houses, Minor Chateaux and Small Churches from the Eleventh to the Sixteenth Century in Normandy, Brittany and Other Parts of France (New York: Architectural Book Publishing Co., 1917)
Fifty Years of Boston (Elizabeth Herlihy, ed.) (Boston: Tercentenary Comm., 1930)
Ghosts, Castles and Victims: Tales of Gothic Horror (J. C. and B. World, eds.) (Greenwich, Conn.: Fawcett, 1974)
Low Cost Suburban Houses (Richardson Wright, ed.) (New York, 1916)

Pamphlets and Printed Addresses

This list is almost certainly very incomplete and is limited to those in the Cram Collection that were found among Mr. Cram's papers.

Architecture and Its Relation to Civilization (Boston: Marshall Jones, Co., 1918)
Address Delivered by Ralph Adams Cram, Litt.D., LL.D., F.R.I.A., A.N.A., F.R.G.S. at the Conference Regarding the Incorporation of St. Hilda's Guild on Corpus Christi, May 30, 1918
The New Middle Ages: Presidential Address Delivered at the Ninth Annual Meeting of the Corporation of the Medieval Academy of America, 28 April, 1934

Journals of Which Cram Was a Founder or Editor

For articles by Cram in same, see *Magazine Articles* below

Knight Errant. A quarterly that first appeared in April, 1892.
Mahogany Tree. A Harvard undergraduate magazine, ca. 1893.
Christian Art. Published in Philadelphia, 1907–09.
Commonweal. First appeared in 1926.
Speculum. The journal of the Medieval Academy of America.

Magazine Articles

This is only a very incomplete list. The relevant collegiate magazines and/or local newspapers and magazines should always be checked at the time Cram churches were dedicated for articles by Cram. One should also check guidebooks to Cram churches, some of which are listed here under *Books about Cram, Goodhue and the Firm's Work*. The 30 May 1928 issue of the *Princeton Alumni Weekly*, for instance (the Chapel Dedication Issue), includes an article by Cram not listed below. It will be the work of many years to hunt all Cram's articles down. The articles listed here are arranged alphabetically by title.

(*American Architect*)

"Architecture as an Expression of Religion," vol. 98, 28 Dec 1910, pp. 209–214, 216–220
"Catalan Arts and Crafts," vol. 130, 5 Aug. 1926, pp. 89–97
"The Case Against the Ecole des Beaux-Arts," vol. 54, 26 Dec. 1896, pp. 107–109
"Domestic Architecture in Spain," vol. 125, 23 Apr. 1924, pp. 371–378
"Influence of the French School on American Architecture," vol. 66, 25 Nov. 1899, pp. 65–66
"Memorial Church of the Good Shepherd," vol. 133, 20 March 1928, pp. 361–368
"The New Boston College," vol. 119, 8 June 1921, pp. 615–618
"A Note on Bryn Athyn Church," vol. 113, 22 May 1918, pp. 709–712
"Princeton Architecture," vol. 96, 21 July 1909, pp. 21–30
"Renaissance in Spain," vol. 125, 28 March 1924, pp. 289–296
"Schools of Instruction in Architecture," vol. 54, 1926, p. 107
"Scrapping the Slums," vol. 114, 25 Dec. 1918, pp. 761–763
"Spanish Notes," vol. 125, 1924, pp. 40, 54, 187–194, 289–296, 371–378
"Spanish Gothic," vol. 125, 27 Feb. 1924, pp. 103–110
"The Value of Precedent in the Practice of Architecture," vol. 126, 17 Dec. 1924, pp. 567–569

(*American Architecture*)

"Catalunan Architecture," Part I, 20 Oct. 1925
"Catalunan Architecture," Part II, 20 Nov. 1925
"Catalunan Architecture," Part III, 20 Jan. 1926
"Catalunan Architecture," Part IV, 5 Apr. 1926
"Mexican Paradox," vol. 6, Feb. 1936, pp. 466–475

"Mystery of Sakkarch," vol. 4, Jan. 1935, pp. 279–296

(*American Church Monthly*)
"The Blessed Sacrament as a Center of Unity," Dec. 1923

(*American Mercury*)
"Back to What Constitution?", vol. 36, Dec. 1935, pp. 385–392
"End to Democracy," vol. 39, Sept. 1936, pp. 23–31
"Invitation To Monarchy," vol. 37, Apr. 1936, pp. 478–486
"Mass-Man Takes Over," vol. 45, Oct. 1938, pp. 166–176
"Radio City, and After," vol. 23, July 1931, pp. 291–296
"White Magic," vol. 19, March 1930, pp. 268–273
"Why Do We Not Behave Like Human Beings," vol. 27, Sept. 1932, pp. 4–18

(*American Review*)
"Chapters from an Autobiography," vol. 5, Oct.–Dec. 1935
"Embargo on Talk," vol. 1, 29 Nov. 1919, pp. 620–621
"Forgotten Class," vol. 7, Apr.–May 1936, pp. 32–46, 179–191
"Fulfillment," vol. 4, March 1935, pp. 513–528
"Nemesis of Democracy," vol. 8, Dec. 1936, pp. 129–141
"Return to Feudalism," vol. 8, Jan. 1937, pp. 336–352

(*Architectural Forum*)
"Architecture Marches On," vol. 70, Feb. 1939, p. 134
"Indianapolis Public Library," vol. 29, 1918, pp. 33–39, 67, 68, 81
"Retrogression in Ugliness: Century of Progress Exposition." vol. 59, July 1923, pp. 24–25

(*Architectural Record*)
"Report of A.I.A. Committee on Education," vol. 31, Feb. 1912, pp. 189–196
"Professor Frothingham's New Volumes," vol. 39, 1916, pp. 290–292
"Lincoln Memorial," vol. 53, Apr. 1923, pp. 478–508
"Religious Aspect of Architecture," vol. 2, Jan.–March 1893, pp. 351–356
"Style in American Architecture," vol. 34, Sept. 1913, pp. 232–239
"War Memorials," vol. 45, Feb. 1919, pp. 116–117
"Work of Cope and Stewardson," vol. 16, Nov. 1904, pp. 407–438
"Work of Frank Miles Day and His Brother," vol. 15, May 1904, pp. 397–421

(*Architectural Review*)
"Early Architecture of Japan," vol. 5, 1898, pp. 54–57
"Good and Bad Modern Gothic Architecture," vol. 6, 1899, pp. 115–119
"Later Architecture of Japan," vol. 5, 1898, pp. 77–80
"A Note on Architectural Style," vol. 12, 1905, pp. 181–195
"John D. Sedding: Some Considerations," vol. 1, 1891, pp. 9–11

(*Architecture*)
"Itolder and Halls, an Appreciation," vol. 37, 1918, pp. 29–52
"John Kirchmayer, Master Craftsman," vol. 63, Feb. 1931, pp. 87–92
"Three Small Chapels," vol. 46, 1922, pp. 363–369

(*Arts and Decoration*)
"America's Beautiful Modern Homes," vol. 21, May 1924, pp. 10–13
"Demonstrating Beauty," vol. 20, Dec. 1923, pp. 13–14
"Limits of Modernism in Art," vol. 20, Jan. 1924, pp. 11–13
"Need for Color in Our Modern Architecture," vol. 20, March 1924, pp. 9–11
"Pre-Eminence of Our Own Domestic Architecture," vol. 22, Apr. 1925, pp. 21–23
"Re-discovery of Quality in Building," vol. 21, Sept. 1924, pp. 16–19
"Reformation of the Art Museum," vol. 21, June 1924, pp. 30–31
"Stained Glass: An Art Restored," vol. 20, Feb. 1924, pp. 11–13

(*Atlantic Monthly*)
"Approach to Religion," vol. 160, Oct. 1937, pp. 469–472
"Cherries of Veno," vol. 85, Apr. 1900, pp. 479–482
"Last of the Squires," vol. 145, Jan. 1930, pp. 80–85
"Second Coming of Art," vol. 119, Feb. 1917, pp. 193–203

(*Barnwell Bulletin*)
"Art and Contemporary Society," vol. 8, Feb. 1931, pp. 17–29

(*Brickbuilder*)
"Ecclesiastical Architecture," vol. 14, 1905, pp. 113–117, 134–140, 164–174
"On the Use of Brick in Domestic Architec-

ture," vol. 4, 1895, pp. 33–52, 99–100, 251–253

(*Catholic World*)
"Pursuit of Ugliness," vol. 130, Feb. 1930, pp. 602–604

(*Christian Art*)
"Architectural Education in the U.S.," vol. I, Apr.–Sept. 1907, pp. 70–74
Editorials: vol. I, Apr.–Sept. 1907, pp. 19, 62, 109, 188, 235, 285; vol. II, Oct. 1907–March 1908, pp. 52, 101, 160, 208, 256, 304; vol. III, Apr.–Sept. 1908, p. 150
"Work of Henry Wilson," vol. 2, 1907–08, pp. 261–273

(*Churchman*)
(Cram's book *Church Building* was serialized in this journal, 1898–99)
"All Saints' Church, Ashmont," vol. XXIX, 15 Apr. 1899, pp. 589–593

(*Commonweal*)
"Change Beyond," vol. 31, 3 Nov. 1939, pp. 33–35
"How Shall We Govern," vol. 16, 13 July 1932, pp. 277–278, 287–288
"Notes on Mexico," vol. 24, 22 May 1936, p. 91
"Recovery or Regeneration," vol. 21, Nov. 1934, pp. 7–10, 56–58
"Reflections upon Art," vol. 10, 5 June 1929, pp. 120–122
"Tangled Towers of Today," vol. 13, 22 Apr. 1931, pp. 673–674
"What Can Be Done for Art," vol. 10, 12 June 1929, pp. 153–155

(*Current Literature*)
"Religious Architecture of Japan," vol. 36, May 1904, pp. 531–536

(*Current Opinion*)
"A Gothic Revival in America," vol. 71, Aug. 1921, pp. 204–206
"Walled Towns in America," vol. 68, Jan. 1920, pp. 82–85

(*Educational Review*)
"Education and the Qualitative Standard," vol. 57, Apr. 1919, pp. 304–311

(*Everybodys*)
"Cathedrals under the War Cloud," vol. 31, Dec. 1914, pp. 782–793

(*Forum*)
"What Is Civilization," vol. 73, March 1925, pp. 350–358

(*Harvard Graduate Magazine*)
"The Test of Beauty," vol. 30, Sept. 1921, pp. 1–20

(*Hibert Journal*, London)
"The Present Need of an Aristocracy," vol. 17, April 1 1919, pp. 371–386

(*House and Garden*)
"Promise of American Building," vol. 29, Jan. 1916, pp. 9–12, 68–70
"Japanese Temple Gardens," vol. 2, 1902, pp. 77–90

(*House Beautiful*)
"Will This Modernism Last," vol. 65, Jan. 1929, p. 45.
"Noteworthy Houses by Well Known Architects," vol. 46, Sept. 1919, pp. 129–132

(*Journal of American Federation of Arts*)
"The Relationship of Architecture to the People," vol. I, 1910, pp. 16–22

(*Journal of Royal Institute of British Architects*)
"Recent University Architecture in the U.S.," vol. 19, 1911–12, pp. 497–518

(*Ladies Home Journal*)
"Country Houses of Moderate Cost," vol. 18, Jan 1901

(*Landscape Architecture*)
"Architecture and England," vol. 114, July 1933, pp. 23–25
"Unity of the Arts," vol. 23, Apr. 1933, pp. 159–163

(*New England Magazine*)
"Bells of Christ Church, Boston," vol. 11, p. 640

(*Poet Lore*)
"Excalibur," vol. 44, no. 4, 1938, pp. 351–362
"Boat of Love," vol. 42, no. 2, 1940, pp. 165–177

(*Pencil Points*)
"Have I a Philosophy of Design," vol. 13, Nov. 1932, pp. 729–734

(*Scribner's Magazine*)
"Rheims and Louvain," vol. 56, Dec. 1914, pp. 814–818

(*Stained Glass*)
"Stained Glass in Church Architecture," vol. 26, July 1931, pp. 223–229

(*Time*)
"Protestantism Is Bankrupt," vol. 27, 6 Jan. 1936, pp. 32–33

(*Western Architect*)
"Architectural Education," vol. 13, Feb. 1909

(*Yale Review*)
"Rheims Cathedral," vol. 8, Oct. 1918, pp. 34–36

7. BIBLIOGRAPHY

Books about Cram, Goodhue and the Firm's Work Not by Cram

Montgomery Schuyler. *The Works of Cram, Goodhue and Ferguson.* New York, *Architectural Record*, entire contents of issue of Jan. 1911 (vol. XXIX, no. 1.)

A Book of Architectural and Decorative Drawings by Bertram Grosvenor Goodhue. New York, The Architectural Book Publishing Co., 1914, 1924

Bertram Grosvenor Goodhue, Architect and Master of Many Arts. New York, A.I.A. Press, 1925.

The Works of Cram and Ferguson, Architects, Including Work by Cram, Goodhue and Ferguson. New York, Pencil Points Press, 1929. (Intro. by Charles Maginnis)

Alfred Tappan North (ed.). *Ralph Adams Cram.* New York, McGraw Hill, 1931

Douglass Shand Tucci. *All Saints Church, Ashmont: An Introduction to the Architecture of Ralph Adams Cram.* Vol. II of *The Gothic Churches of Dorchester.* Boston, Tribune Publishing Co. (second printing, University Microfilms, Ann Arbor, Mich., 1975)

Douglass Shand Tucci. *Church Building in Boston: With an Introduction to the Work of Ralph Adams Cram and the Boston Gothicists.* Concord, N.H., Rumford Press for the Trustees of The Dorchester Savings Bank, 1975

Ann Miner Daniel. *The Early Ecclesiastical Architecture of Ralph Adams Cram.* 1976, Ph.D. thesis, University of North Carolina at Chapel Hill

A number of books have naturally been written about specific churches by the firm. Among those that deal with the firm's work at some length or even entirely the following may be noted.

St. Paul's Cathedral, 100 Years. Detroit, 1924. (Two chapters were written by Cram)

Milo Hudson Gates. *A Description of the Chapel of the Intercession, Trinity Parish, New York.* New York, 1931

Harold E. Grove. *St. Thomas Church.* New York, 1965

Edward H. Hall. *A Guide to The Cathedral Church of St. John The Divine in the City of New York* (17th ed.) New York, 1965

Richard Stillwell. *The Chapel of Princeton University.* Princeton, N.J., Princeton University Press, 1971

Douglass Shand Tucci. *All Saints', Ashmont, Dorchester, Boston: A Centennial History.* Boston, 1975.

Douglass Shand Tucci. *Treasures: A Guide to Stained Glass and Architectural Sculpture at The Cathedral Church of St. John The Divine in New York.* New York, 1976

George W. Wickersham. *Crossroads: A History of The Cathedral Church of St. John The Divine in New York.* New York, 1976